DAY TRADING:

The Basic Beginners Guide To Learn How To Trade For A Living, Swing Market Tools, Forex Tactics & Secrets, Psychology and Discipline On How To Profit And Become An Intelligent Trader

By Matthew Stock

© **Copyright 2020 - All rights reserved.**

The content contained within this book may not be reproduced, duplicated or transmitted without direct written permission from the author or the publisher.

Under no circumstances will any blame or legal responsibility be held against the publisher, or author, for any damages, reparation, or monetary loss due to the information contained within this book. Either directly or indirectly.

Legal Notice:

This book is copyright protected. This book is only for personal use. You cannot amend, distribute, sell, use, quote or paraphrase any part, or the content within this book, without the consent of the author or publisher.

Disclaimer Notice:

Please note the information contained within this document is for educational and entertainment purposes only. All effort has been executed to present accurate, up to date, and reliable, complete information. No warranties of any kind are declared or implied. Readers acknowledge that the author is not engaging in the rendering of legal, financial, medical or professional advice. The content within this book has been derived from various sources. Please consult a licensed professional before attempting any techniques outlined in this book.

By reading this document, the reader agrees that under no circumstances is the author responsible for any losses, direct or indirect, which are incurred as a result of the use of information contained within this document, including, but not limited to, — errors, omissions, or inaccuracies.

Table of Contents

Introduction **5**

Chapter 1 What is Day Trading **12**

Chapter 2 Pros and Cons of Day Trading **26**

Chapter 3 What a Beginner Needs to Know **31**

Chapter 4 Wall Street **37**

Chapter 5 What is Best to Trade? **48**

Chapter 6 Trading Basic Concepts **56**

Chapter 7 Average Income of a Day Trader **60**

Chapter 8 Trading Strategies and Techniques **74**

Chapter 9 Investing Opportunities **88**

Chapter 10 What Kind of Day Trader are You **101**

Chapter 11 Managing Risk in Trading and the Role of Journaling **118**

Chapter 12 Tips For Market Investing **132**

Conclusion **142**

Introduction

Getting started with day trading is a pretty big decision. You can achieve the ideal of bringing in profits with only a few hours a day trading, but that will not be the reality for many people that are just beginners, because it will be necessary to just stay above the water during the first year and to get a feel for what it is like with all the fluctuations. Your only goal during the beginning and the learning stages is to just stay in the game and not to sink. If you still want to undertake this activity, and if you are still interested after this introduction, then day trading just might be for you. It is necessary to have the right knowledge, to get anywhere.

You cannot be superficial when doing day trading, you need to have a plan and a certain strategy to have an advantage. Do not take any trade too lightly and always have an open mind. You should try to locate a live chart for a certain asset you have a decent knowledge base for, and you should watch how the value of that asset changes over time. As you are paying attention to that asset, you should be considering how you would enter that trade and also, how you would exit it. You should also be aware of your level of accepted risk that you are willing to undertake. Moreover, you should also know how many assets you are willing to hold. These are just some of the main considerations.

However, have a consistent strategy so that you can monitor your results and see what works and what does not over time. You can ask someone to provide you with a strategy or you can figure it out yourself by observing an asset and the changes in its value.

Being a practitioner by trying things out and practicing, is what will get you success in the game of day trading. If you want to be good at anything, such as public speaking, you have to practice and go through repetition. Only by practice, you can get good and wise and above all get knowledge. It is good to have a separate account that will be used just for practice and experimentation before you start day trading for real. The fact is that every trader is different than the other, and the circumstances always change, therefore the only solution is to practice and to have a strategy that you can rely on.

You have to get in fact, well acquainted with the strategy you are currently working with since you will want to be able to take good instinctive decisions and not over think small things when real capital is on the line. One more advice, do not go into trading for real until you have managed to make a profit with your practicing account.

For you to get started in day trading, you should know how much capital you need. You can look at capital like you would look at employees and how good you would be at managing your capital, will determine the money you will be making.

Whichever amount of capital you decide to start trading with, you will want to give yourself a safety net and deposit a little more money than the initial amount, around 20% more. It is good to have this as a measure since there are rules and restrictions. For instance, in the example of trading stocks, you will not be able to get into and get out of the trade during the same day, if events start to unfold contrary to what you expected as a part of your strategy.

When you look at forex, for example, the minimum amount of capital for entering does not truly exist, but you still want to have a decent amount of capital, since very little capital means that you do not have a lot of opportunities and a lot of possible plays.

Whichever option you go with, it will not be easy and it will be necessary to have starting capital in dollars instead of pennies. Your strategy should include certain restrictions and fail-safes. You constantly have to be evaluating your situations such as whether you have enough capital to go through with what you want to do. It is better to wait instead of going on without being sufficiently prepared. Also, certain trades can require you to set aside a couple of hours each day and you should plan for that. If you are working a job alongside with day trading, then you have to be aware of what time of the day you will be able to trade actively, as it will influence your strategy and overall circumstances of the trade. You need to design your trading strategy around your situation. The amount of time that you put in, is ultimately up to you and the speed at which you can get to your desired level of income, will depend on how many hours you are willing to dedicate.

When you are ready to start, you will need to find yourself a broker. This is probably a more important decision than any other trade that you will be making since this person will be handling your capital and your livelihood. When making a decision about which broker you will choose, you have to look for a combination of him being reputable, having an acceptable fee, and customer service.

Day trading is not something which you can make money with overnight, so you will have to commit to mastery, that is done through settling on a strategy, and then consistently practicing that strategy, until you can prove that it can net you a profit. You should first be able to make a profit with your dummy account so that once you feel confident, you can hire a broker and move on to bigger things.

Below is the list of pros and cons of day trading which you can use to additionally realize if day trading is something you wish to take part in. Some of the upsides of going into day trading are:

There are no barriers to entry as far as education or certification are concerned. The interesting thing is that many successful day traders, do not have extensive formal education, but even if they were to have, it is unlikely that they would have learned something that they could quickly apply to get some real-world results. Actually, the long-winded education system would probably have you, as a consequence, over thinking stuff and not taking action since you are just sitting down and absorbing information without applying it any time soon. This all means that you are in control of your time and you can choose when you will work and when you will not. Markets are open from business pretty much all of the time and this is something that is constant across all categories of trading. More possibilities and more flexibility always come in handy. Freedom may be the only reason why you want to get into day trading and that is perfectly fine and that is a pretty good reason.

To make things even more accessible, you only need a working internet connection and a computer of any kind, preferably a laptop, so that you can be on the move. These resources are getting more and more affordable and therefore they do not present a barrier of entry.

Another benefit is the fact that day trading can lead you to earn a nice profit if you are good and if you are well aware of what you are doing. If you can recognize a good market and if you can catch on changes in prices and values, then you can earn pretty good money even in a day. Still, this will not be a matter of luck or lottery and it will not be something that can be done without training.

The choice of the market in which you will be doing your business is ultimately yours. There is a variety of markets in which you can take part in, that make you capable of recognizing which market can lead you to achieve the largest success. So, you should choose a couple of markets and then, you should really seek to understand them so that, you can become an expert and get a feel for their pulse and their movements.

However, there are still some downsides that should be considered, and those are listed below:

Even though you can have freedom by doing day trading, there can still be a requirement for time investment and especially if you want to focus. If you focus on a couple of markets to understand them better, it can take you as much time as a standard 40-hour workweek would, and you also may not get anything contrary to getting a fixed salary. You can always invest less of your time, but then, you are quite unlikely to achieve results that can positively impact your life.

The risk of losing your money is always present in day trading, this does not happen when you have a permanent job. Just because you put your capital into something, that does not mean it will bring you some profit or even a breakup. One way to mitigate it is to switch to binary options and by doing so, you know completely how much can risk and how much you can lose, in the worst case, even if the costs of trading are higher in this situation which means that the profit will be in some lower way. However, this small profit is the price that many people are ready to pay to be sure of the risk and how much they can lose. In this way, you take measured and calculated risks.

Just like any skill, day trading requires time and patience to learn and to get good at it. You must have reasonable expectations, and you have to take a more long term view, to realize that you will not be using day trading to quit your job the following week. You should be prepared for the fact that it will take you a year to learn the process. I would like to be able to say that a weekend course, would be all that is required to start bringing in the cash, but that would make me a liar.

Chapter 1

What is Day Trading

What is Day Trading?

Day trading is basically the purchasing and selling of securities within a single trading day in any common marketplace, stock markets and foreign exchange (FOREX), to obtain a compound of short term loans. Day traders who are involved in this, are fully investing in this trading activity with multiple learning sources. Learning time and a good kind of capital often end up being successful. Being successful in day trading literally means acquiring large chunks of profits amounts.

Characteristics of a Day Trader

Being a day trader does come out naturally. Moreover, a specific personality and some traits are duly required. Below are some of the characteristics of a day trader.

Disciplined.

This is a major trait that day traders really need to input. Day traders should always be disciplined to remain input when no opportunities emerge and should act faster when opportunities avail. Acting fast also includes strictly considering the step by step rules and obligations initially formed in their big plans.

Open-minded.

Day trading is a learning kind of income-generating engagement, implying that there are going to be happy times and the downfalls. Save yourself and learn from all that. Improve the happy times and completely discard the downfall of wrong moves. Being exposed to the winnings and the failures makes you open-minded, and a master of all possible win moves.

A fan of technology.

Day trading is carried out in various trading platforms and systems that a trader should be familiarized with. This should not scare you. Getting to know how they work does not, in any case, require you to be a computer whiz. Get to learn the basic moves and grow technologically with time.

Mentally tough.

Losing market trades are constant; most of the successful traders will have losing trades every single day. But, will slightly win more times than they lose. It is so important to stay focused and be rational during a losing period, but most of all, do not let in the basic fact that money has been lost too. Focus on the future day trading activities by implementing some of the strategies outlined in a big plan.

Independence.

Independence is striving to build your own toolbox that will always guide you along your path. Reading many trading books, watching every video, interacting with one mentor after the other, can be considered a total miss. What if different books have one confusing point on a particular field? What if your YouTube subscriber decides to quit vlogging? Always grasp the basics after in-depth research and then keep your guard up. Dare yourself to prove your courage, and get large chunks of benefits. However, when you feel you are so lost, do not hesitate to get assistance. Most importantly, master and analyze successful moves and let them be part of your big plan.

Patience.

Good things do take quite some time. In every strategical move, you try to make, think about it carefully, but this should not make you paranoid. Act accordingly with many disciplines, to reduce the number of losses likely to be incurred during various day trading activities.

Also, a patient day trader is a learning day trader. Day trading is not going to be easy at first, but with time and practice, will gain lots of skills and experience, so things will be expected to flow very smoothly. Hey, be patient!

Future-oriented.

Getting stuck in the past makes you much of a prisoner. Forward-thinking lets you see the possible moves and gives you the decisive air when the next trading activity will occur, considering the set protocols set in the day trader's plan. Being future-oriented incites forward-thinking, which above all involves mental thinking, leading you to know your next possible moves after a considerate examination. Being future-oriented hastens and simplifies the day trading operation moves, so that chances are going to be more successful.

Financial freedom.

Day trading does not require you to be necessarily a tycoon, but it requires to have a specific amount of money that has been precisely selected to begin day trading with. Remember the first times are always a win or loss situation as you continue to learn and grow. This particular set of money can be lost too. Be careful about how you handle your finances in day trading. Not every story is a good story.

Enthusiasm.

A great interest in something is a pending successful goal. A great enthusiastic inclination to stocks, securities, commodities, markets, and business, gives you the thirst to learn and master what day trading is all about. These are signs of a future successful day trader.

Experience and familiarity.

Experience comes with pretty much of downfall lessons and learning. Expose yourself to different learning sources and master every profitable move during day trading, to squeeze out the best of that. Getting the better experience and familiarity of the trading platforms and various strategies needed to be successful at day trading is worthwhile.

Difference between Long and Short Trade

In stock markets, the terms long and short basically imply whether a trade was initiated by first selling or first purchasing. A long trade starts when the day trader purchases at a particular price, and to sell at a higher price in the future, in a bid to get profits. Whereas short trades start with selling, before even purchasing with the intent to repurchase at a lower price from the market, and eventually acquire profits.

Short selling is simply:
- Borrow the stock.
- Sell the stock.
- Buyback the stock?
- Profit or loss?

Risks are also involved during short selling; stock prices may end up being so high and normally, there is no limit to how a particular price can actually go.

During long trading, your profit potential is unlimited since the price of the asset can rise indefinitely.

Can One Do Day Trading for a Living?

The first point to take down is yes, day trading is a lucrative engagement. However, that does not mean that it is way more simple than any other actual job. And yes, you get to be your boss. You get to do it your way, on your time, with your strategies for a living. It is amazing! We do not get so lucky in this life though, because drawbacks have to appear too. Below, let us venture on the different pros and cons that come with day trading.

Benefits:

- Own boss

Getting to work the way you desire, has always been the best thing ever. Your plan, your moves, your strategies. This is so great! Imagine going for a wanting vacation without first passing through the Human Resource department, with some great explanation so that your reason can be valid enough. Moreover, getting to work on your own, already gives you the full energy to make things alive. You have enough spirit to learn and bring the best in and out of you. Do yourself a huge favor, and be your boss.

- Comfort.

A peaceful working environment enhances the quality of the end product, or rather, the aftermath turns out to be so successful. A peaceful environment creates a more-concentrated workspace, day traders get to strictly master the actual day trading activities, and learn more every day. This will, in the end, accomplish their big plans as indicated by the large chunks of profits that would be made.

- Risk management.

Exposure day by day cases of day trading will make you a better risk-taker. Day trading is made up of so many risks, that act as everyday lessons. The trader gets to master the good moves and discard the previously made mistakes to become a successful day trader.

- Technologically advantaged.

Day trading exposes you to the internet as you try to get access to various sources. The internet is technology, and it is full of advanced technologies. You are exposed to new sites and different technological techniques. This builds you because technology is the present and the future.

Drawbacks:

- A solitary lifestyle.

Day trading is a peace of mind activity implying that physical noise should not be part of it. This creates a lonely kind of environment, since the trader is mostly by his or her self, trying to master the possible good moves. You are going to enjoy day trading if the best company is normally just your company.

- Inconsistent salary figure.

Your smart trading work will be reflected by the salary figure you obtain every single trading day. When you decide to take a day off, no gains are promised. At one particular point, you may gain like $3000, and the next day you experience $2000 loss, no consistent salary figures are promised, your smart moves are the ones that will get you a Lamborghini.

How to Decide on What and When to Buy

When and what exactly to buy in day trading is so fundamental. Let us outline some of the factors that need to be considered.

Understand the level of risk is involved and what kind of risk level is suitable for you.

There is a lot of stocks to trade with different rates of volatility, price, and volume characteristics. There are different kinds of risks experienced in each level of day trading. As a beginner, choose the risk level that matches your risk management rate. Day to day trading activities exposes you to several kinds of risks that occur frequently, so every trading day becomes a learning day. With time, a beginner is exposed to all kinds of possible risks that are likely to be educative, and he or she gets to be a pro in handling risks.

Analyze and come up with the right kinds of prices to buy.

Your personality describes you and therefore, judging from it, you should favor yourself with the kind of day market you want to get involved in. For instance, if you have a fast mind, you can focus on the string of actions needed at a particular circumstance, then you should go for short term trading.

Focus and analyze a particular stock.

Keep it simple. Deal with a particular stock at a time. Understand how it is handled, explore all its sides, and examine how it is operated at multiple time frames. Every stock has its characteristics and personality, meaning that you need to understand its behavior to anticipate the right moves.

Explore several trading charts to understand the stock movement and the overall market performances.

Charts act as a pictorial representation of the actual activities, that are taking place in the day trading market. They help to monitor and convey every moment. A beginner is obliged to master and learn every move that is depicted from the charts, for future successful moves in day trading.

Be disciplined and strictly stay stick with your plan.

Strictly following up the initial strategical set plan is a successful move-in day trading. Being disciplined enough to follow what was examined and noted down as a step, guarantees the day trader the zero chances of incurring a large number of losses.

Time frame.

Traders spend almost 30 seconds in choosing a time frame, not because of their trading technique or trading market, but just because of their personality. For instance, traders that forsee to make so many trades during the day, they end up choosing shorter time frames. While on the other hand, traders that intend to make from two to three trades in a particular trading day, they pick longer time frames. Time frames are not constant in the trading day, since the activeness of the trader on that particular day, says it all.

Deciding When to Sell

Mental fatigue.

Brain fatigue incites poor trading performances that correspond to long strings of stop losses. Trading for just two or three hours, keeps you set in your game and the chances of excelling in your trading activities, are pretty much high.

Trading at the opening.

It is recommendable for beginners not to engage in the first 15 minutes of a new trading day. It is believed, by most seasoned traders, that during this period, a lot of dumb money is initiated. Dumb money is simply the actual amount of capital that most traders use, as they sell and buy market prices based on the immediate previous trading episodes during the start of their trading day. Professional day traders are advantaged in this particular morning.

Ending trading by 11.30 pm and 10.30 am ET is considered to be the best day trading period. It offers the biggest moves in the shortest amount of time. Well, you can also decide to extend one more hour since that is when volatility and volume tend to tamper off.

The last hour

Most traders are likely to trade the last hour, which is from 3 pm to 4 pm ET. This period is recommended because most traders have had a long break session since then, and are likely to have resurfaced and focused. The last hour is much like the first hour, where a lot of dumb money can be depicted as many traders try to unfold on how the day will end up based on the trend during the day. The last hour of the day can be very active with such big moves on high volumes.

Best day and month.

A lot recommend that Friday might be the best day to trade before that Monday dip happens, mostly, if it is the first Friday of the month or when it precedes a three-day weekend.

Risks Involved in Day Trading

Financial breakdown.

It is so advisable that you interact with the kind of capital that you are ready to lose. Due to the meager time frame during day trading, prices fluctuate from time to time. The amount you traded with, is not so predictable, and it can be easily subjected to a major loss. Be careful with how you handle your finances, the financial breakdown can be a possible option as well.

Also, day traders must payday trade firms commissions, and tutorial costs to be subjected to the trainers. Day trading is cost-effective.

Margin borrowing.

Margin borrowing basically is the loan amount you acquire for the essence of purchasing securities. The amount is likely to grow from the impacted interest, and potentially put the trader in a position of over-borrowing. It is highly recommended that the trader should clearly understand how margin borrowing goes about, before trading on borrowed capital.

Market movements.

The market moves in less than a hundred points in either direction, in a single trading day. Traders normally spot every market move and are likely to acquire higher rates of profits. Therefore, they can observe and act on several happening moves. After all, they may be successful. Being late on a trade can convert a potential profit to a loss. Try to stay updated on what is happening in the trade market.

Psychological addiction.

Day trading is considered to have the same weigh as that of gambling. Day trading is highly addictive since, the traders are said to eventually turn out competitive, and of above-average intelligence.

Slippage risk.

This kind of risk involves hidden costs that are normally associated with every transaction. It normally takes place anytime in the market, but mostly when you are using orders during high volatile times. It also occurs, when you place huge orders on assets with less interest in purchasing. Slippage risks mostly affect forex, and stock traders in the market. Try your best to avoid slippage risks by using limit orders in trading, rather than market orders.

Risks of over-trading.

Overtrading occurs in several circumstances. You may incur over trading in the aspect of trying to recover for the made losses. Another way, you may try to average your position, when stop losses are approaching, and end up causing over-trading. Try to avoid such risks in all aspects.

Stock selection.

Stock selection is so fundamental in day trading. If you get your stock selection wrong, it is not going to be beneficial for you. So, select stocks that are quite liquid and exhibit clear trading patterns that are going to work for you. Wrong stock selection, incurs large amounts of losses which will most probably diminish you.

Technical analysis.

Technical analysis is not a perfect science. Assumptions that past patterns are likely to repeat are never good assumptions, and in many cases incur to major risk of stop losses, triggering on either side of the trade.

Market volatility.

Market volatility is the norm in market day trading. Even with your best-set strategies and well-picked kind of stock, day trading episodes are not often predictable. External macro factors at day trading make the market volatile, triggering a string of stop losses and, after all, you end up putting your day trading capital at a bigger risk.

Emotional trading.

Again, a failing plan is planning to fail. Some of the day traders target the hot stocks that are probably recommended by several spam email reports, in believing in acquiring major profits. Okay, a turn of events is likely to unfold. Day trading is a kind of systematic income-generating activity. A strategical plan with major points to note when handling day trading should be formulated. It ought to guide you on several major day trading moves, mistakes, and their solutions, with updated keywords that he or she learn as they keep on working on day trading.

Trading with small amounts.

There is a limit that has been set to day trading. Slightly bigger limits are recommended to avoid many risks from being incurred.

Chapter 2

Pros and Cons of Day Trading

Advantages of Day Trading

Our book title already specified that we are going to be exploring day trading. As such, any trades that you will open, whether in cryptocurrency, forex, binary options, options, ETFs, or futures, will be closed on the same day. I have been trading for well over a decade, and I had to try all the four trading styles before settling on day trading. My conclusion was that scalping was too tiresome and risky, not to mention the emotional overload after placing several-second trades. Swing and position trading, on the other hand, was too boring for an impatient person like me, who had to pay his bills from trading only.

Here are some of the reasons that I chose to go for day trading.

Ease of Getting Started

Day trading only requires a person to have the skills, a computer or smartphone, some little money, and a comfortable workstation. Getting the skills is as easy as finding a mentor who has been in the industry for some time (like you did by purchasing this book) and, let them show you the profitable methods. You can also do it, through practice and experience by reading tons of books and watching videos. However, this can be time-consuming and expensive since most of the information out there is too vague.

Further, since the trade positions held by a day trader are small, you do not need a lot of money to get started. Swing and position trading aims at riding huge price movements, which also come with the burden of sourcing for enough capital. With day trading, though, all you need is a few dollars, and you will be on your way to earning from trading.

Fewer Risks

The second advantage of day trading is that there are fewer risks involved. First, due to the short time required for holding positions, one is advised to risk only a small percentage of their account. If eventually, losses occur, only a small amount is lost. Second, in day trading, you can open several positions within a day. As such, if some of the positions become losers, they can be closed and the profitable ones left to run. On the contrary, swing and position traders usually have very few trade opportunities. Therefore, when the trades turn into losers, they have no winning trades to cover the loss.

Daily Profits

How does it feel to end every day with your salary already paid? This is possible with day trading. Since all trades need to be closed by the end of the day, you will know how much you made or lost before going to bed. Day traders, therefore, have more peace of mind compared to long-term traders who might need to wait for days or months before knowing the fate of their trades.

More Opportunities

Once we start analyzing the charts, you will understand this better. Traders use what we call "timeframes" to analyze their charts. Scalpers use the least timeframes, which might be as low as 1 minute up to 5 minutes. Therefore, in a day, they can find tens or hundreds of opportunities. Day traders use 15-minute charts up to 1 hour, meaning they get tens of opportunities. When it comes to the larger timeframes, such as daily, weekly, and monthly, trading opportunities might be fewer.

Fewer Transaction Costs

You need to understand that brokers charge a tiny amount of money for providing traders with market data, and trading platforms. Whenever you make a trade, a little amount is charged. You will notice that some brokers charge an extra amount for trades that stay overnight. As such, a trade that runs for many days will be charged something daily. In the long run, the amount might accumulate and reduce one's profits or capital. Day traders, however, are not charged since they do not have sleepover trades.

Familiarity with the Markets

The last advantage of day trading is that since the learner she or he spends a lot of time on the charts, they get to familiarizes themselves with the movements of prices in the markets. In short, they get to understand the individual instruments that they are trading. I have found this to be true since I know how some stocks and currencies behave when the markets open before important news releases and before prices start to change. All these have helped to increase my earnings and reduce my losses.

Disadvantages of Day Trading

I like to be honest about everything. In light of this, let me reveal that while day trading might appear to be the perfect trading style, it has disadvantages of its own.

Let us look at them.

Higher Chances of Making Losses

Day trading can be very risky, especially for unskilled or uninformed traders. Since we make numerous trades within a day, if all of them or a majority of them were losers, it would cause significant harm to your account. Do not worry, though, because this book is meant to make you informed, so you can remain on the profitable side.

Tedious

Trading is a very interesting profession since you get to sit down, analyze charts, and watch as your money grows. However, when it is overdone, it can be tedious, just like anything else. Every trade requires proper analysis; so, the more trades that you make, the more likely you are to burn out. This can be avoided by setting specific times for trading and having a few instruments to analyze.

Price Fluctuations

The prices of all financial instruments change every microsecond. The rate of change might differ across markets.

For example, stocks fluctuate less than currencies. The rate of change becomes more noticeable as one uses lower timeframes to do their analysis. That said, a day trader can be surprised by sudden price fluctuations due to unexpected economic events, and this might lead to losses. On the other hand, swing and position traders are less affected by changes in prices because they use larger timeframes, which fluctuate less.

As we have seen, traders have four trading styles which to choose from. This can be determined by many factors. In our case, we have decided to go for day trading, since the aim of this guide is to help you make a living out of online trading. Day trading is the only style that you can set daily targets, and know how much you will be earning in a month. Besides, it provides you with the chance to recover your losses since it provides tens of opportunities every day. Concisely, if you make losses today, you will still have more opportunities to recover them tomorrow. Swing trading provides fewer opportunities, and this might not be the most suitable trading style to achieve continuous cash flow.

Chapter 3

What a Beginner Needs to Know

The in-depth understanding of day trading cannot be achieved only from its mere definition. There is still more that encompasses day trading, that you would require to know and understand before regarding yourself as an expert in day trading. Especially for you as a beginner, the journey is still long, but with a clear mindset and focus, you will soon get to understand everything that revolves around day trading and be fully proficient. With day trading, it is absolutely possible to earn good pay for very few hours within a day. However, individuals who get into the market without a clear understanding of day trading, always end up getting enormous losses.

Having a strategy, you will realize that for all the various methods of carrying out any trade, require a certain strategy. You ought to adopt or rather create one that best suits you. You may risk a failure, making huge losses in your trade. Day trading is not just like any other kind of trade, which you would just succeed in a whim without a clear strategy. You need to ask yourself various questions like: "how will you get into the trade?", "what do you need to have to get into the trade?", or still "how much in terms of profits do you think you will get?" "how many shares of stock would you purchase with the money that you have set aside for the day trade?", "how much would you stand to lose in case things go haywire?"

Having these questions in mind, they will act as driving forces towards the know-how of starting the trade. Implementing them, once you are in the trade, gives you a kind of a method that you can try out over and over again. Analyze your results, and find out whether it works in your favor or not. You can also develop a strategy from other people as well, who have been in the trade, and have tried and worked for them.

To be successful in day trade, you will require to do as much practice as possible, especially before you decide on using your own hard-earned money in the trade. As the old saying goes, "practice makes perfect". You do not necessarily have to have high educational qualifications to make it in day trading. Practice hard to find that one strategy that suits you. The practice here is using demo accounts. The idea is to make much practice as possible in total liberty, to try out your most recently learned strategy, and see whether it works out well for you. When you find yourself being profitable in a demo account, then from there on, you can decide to get into real trading. Use the same strategy that you have been using in your demo account. The idea here of practicing as much as possible, to spot repeating patterns. However, the demo account, to some extent, may not be similar to real trading, in terms of the pressures and associated risks, but it still plays a critical role in ensuring that you acquire the necessary confidence and understand better your best trading method. Due to this, at first, you may realize that your trade might not end up as well as you expected, as it was when you practiced the demo. This should not worry you and cause you any kind of problem. It is so natural and is expected. The choice of the demo account would, to some extent, also matter considering that some do not expire; hence, they provide you with an opportunity to trade as much as you would wish to.

The issue of the amount of capital that you would require to get into the trade, is also a key factor. This determines how much you get as returns in case of profits within a day of trading. The minimum amount to start with may be specific with some markets, while others do not have a set minimum. The majority of the traders, on the other hand, only put in the capital that they can afford to lose. Somehow this helps eliminate emotions, while in the trade hence, enable them to make sound decisions. Moreover, having very low capital for your day trade may disadvantage you as you may end up paying extremely high commissions while at the same time receiving poor order executions. You will realize that all markets usually offer good profit potential. Furthermore, the only factor that stands out is the amount of capital you invest — putting these into consideration, having a large capital to trade with, stands out as an added advantage in Day Trading. Nonetheless, do not be misguided into believing that day trading is one quick, easy way of making money overnight. This only applies when you are well aware of the trade; have defined clear strategies and a deep understanding of your market. Moreover, despite the many skills, luck in one way or another, as well as good timing skills, counts.

You also need to understand that for a day trade, you will require to have a broker. Your choice of a broker is quite critical, as this is the person whom you will have to trust the most, as you will invest all of your capital. Here you may decide to settle with the online broker whom you opened the demo account with, or choose another one. The majority of the day traders usually prefer those brokers who base their charges per share, instead of per trade. In the case where a broker charges high commissions, then he can negatively affect your profitability based on your day's strategy despite you wanting to save your profits by looking for low fee brokers. You have to ensure that they are quite reliable; otherwise, you may end up losing a lot of your dollars. It would also be advisable to seek the services of those brokers who provide you with the opportunity to place multiple orders.

You also need to know when you should be carrying out your trade. The consistency in this, not only works for the beginners but the pros as well. You will not have to necessarily spend the whole day trading. The best way to achieve this consistency is to trade for say two to three hours. It is also essential to understand the best time to focus on doing your trades based on market volatility. Try knowing when the price moves are quite sizable and offer the best potential profit.

It would be wise to understand how to manage your risks. This involves the day's risks as well as the trading risks. For trade risks, you can reduce them to as much as 1% for each trade. This can be achieved by setting a stop loss. This will remove you from the trade, in case you start losing significantly. For the day's risk, you understand that one single day can ruin your entire week or even month! Setting it at around 3% of your entire capital is quite manageable. This protects you from being emotional, as you make decisions in the trade as well; no matter how strong you may think you are when faced with enormous losses, your psychology always starts making hopeless and fruitless decisions that end up ruining your trade completely. Being affected emotionally by your trade is a clear indication that you are trading too much money. Day trading is more of betting, making bets in a way that the probability of winning is to your advantage, then is your ultimate success in day trade. However, the magnitude of the percentage loss that you decide on taking, can change depending on the number of wins that you get as compared to the losses. If the wins are many and give high returns, then setting your stop loss a bit high would only work better for you as that would translate to higher profits. The idea of managing your risks is to make your losses quite small such as that one single day of winning can compensate for the accrued losses.

You may have in mind the market that would interest you to trade. You should be in a position to find a repeating pattern that would be quite convenient to exploit and make profits from. As earlier indicated, no market is better than the other. What differentiates is your capital investment and what exactly you want to trade. You realize that some markets may vary depending on the time of operation, e.g., for forex, it runs 24/7. In others, they do not charge any commissions. Other markets have high volatility; hence, the traders enjoy huge trade swings. This may work both as an advantage or a disadvantage since theses swing also mean enormous risks of huge losses. Do not take the risk to try to master all the markets that come your way. You just need to focus on one to avoid having divided attention. The moment you learn to make profits from one of the markets, it becomes easier to master the rest.

Chapter 4

Wall Street

Once in the past, Wall Street was necessary for stock trading. People would flock to the market, yell out numbers for trades their clients wanted, and prices would fluctuate as more and more buyers and sellers traded for the day. The ticker boards were not automated, instead, they were handwritten, changing every few seconds.

Phones would be ringing. Voices would be yelling to be heard over the din. But then, computers came along. For the generations in their late thirties, who had many advancements in computers, from the personal home computer became available, to the internet, it seems impossible that in the mid-

1900s computers were being used. They were just too large to be in the average home.

As computers were scaled down to more manageable sizes, Wall Street gained electronic tickers, computers for investing, and a more streamlined process. During the eighties, Wall Street was using computers to make trades and to connect around the world. But, still, the people and the process were necessary. Most people still did not have computers, although more businesses were making them available.

Things have changed. For those who lived it and were not born after the internet reveal, we know 1994 and the coming decade changed everything. Suddenly, we had access to information from around the globe. We could converse with people half a world away. We could even see stock market information, in real-time, and not from a newspaper.

Today, Wall Street is less necessary for the individual trader. But Wall Street does not want you to understand this point. They do not want the average investor to realize they do not need a financial adviser or a direct line to Wall Street brokers, standing on a floor yelling. What they need are information and strategy.

Why Wall Street want you to understand the new process that is at your fingertips? Why are they trying to keep the secrets of how to trade?

Money

Most things come down to money. Wall Street would lose billions of dollars if the average investor learned how to trade stocks. At least this is what they want you to believe.

The truth is somewhat murky. Yes, Wall Street makes money off your money. When you invest in 401Ks, Wall Street is making the most money. When you place a trade using a financial adviser, there are fees. Fees that pay the adviser, but there are also fees going to Wall Street.

Wall Street gets a cut of what you invest. When you use leverage and do margin trades, Wall Street gains even more. If you change how the cycle works, then Wall Street makes less.

However, there are still fees being paid. Each time a trade is placed, there is a fee. The trading fee can be as little as $5, no matter how much money you invest. The real change from when you choose stocks instead of using a Wall Street adviser comes from leverage, margins, and 401Ks. Your money in the 401K does make money when the stocks increase, which requires more trading of those stocks between individuals and those companies. When a person buys a stock, the demand goes up. When there are hundreds of the same stock, the demand increases. When media companies run news stories that show a company is strong and growing, the stock goes up because of demand increases. Do you understand how it works? It all comes down to supply and demand.

With investments like 401Ks, hedge funds, and mutual funds, you give money to make money, but your money is also being used for leverage, so the companies can make bigger investments. So, consequently, when these investments pay off, you make money.

Let's consider a savings account. You are investing in your future, with an interest rate, such as 1% on the money in your savings account, but the bank is using that money to increase their investments to make money off of you. 401Ks are similar. Your money is making someone else even more money. Hence, this is the reason why Wall Street does not want you to start taking more control of your investments and seeking out the better stocks.

Examining the Parts of Wall Street

Beyond being a symbol, Wall Street is not just one big entity. It is a huge financial system that encompasses banks, securities, and hedge funds. Stocks are traded on the New York Stock Exchange or NYSE. It is only a portion of Wall Street because you also have the Federal Reserve Bank, NASDAQ, Goldman Sachs, JP Morgan Chase, and NYMEX.

With more than one part making up Wall Street, one must understand that stock investing is a portion of the financial markets. You also have the bond market, commodities, futures, and the foreign exchange market. The original purpose of the securities market was to help companies grow, become profitable, and furthermore they provide jobs.

While money can be lost when more individual traders enter the market, there is still plenty to do out there. What is lost are the big commissions, and while that could turn into billions of dollars, there is every reason that the entire financial market – the symbol Wall Street stands for – will not disappear.

What this means, is that you need to gain an education into how the system works, just a small one, and then you can start to assess why investing and by choosing your own stocks is the wiser choice.

Popular Markets for Day Trading

A fundamental part of each day trader's strategic plan is selecting a market or markets to invest in. Most traders are skilled by focusing their efforts on a couple of markets. This permits them to become thoroughly acquainted with the subtleties and idiosyncrasies of the market to allow them to make smarter decisions. Well, known markets for day trading consist of financial futures, foreign currency (or Foreign exchange), and the stock market.

A futures contract is an agreement with the buyer and seller to make a specific trade in a specified future price and date. Standard futures contracts deal with goods, such as foods, fats and oils, fibers and textiles, metals, silver and gold, and miscellaneous items like steer hides and rubber. Investors utilize futures to offset uncertainty and risk. The popular exchanges include the **New York Stock Exchange (NYSE) and Nasdaq**

Other Types of Exchanges

The American Stock Exchange is the third-largest stock market in the U.S. However, in different parts of the world there is a high percentage of stock exchanges that do a lot of business as well, besides the American one. The London Stock Exchange and the Hong Kong Stock Exchange are prime examples of stock exchanges that do a good deal of trading business.

The thing to remember when you are going to be trading is this: that stock prices fluctuate daily because of the market forces out there. That means that it all comes down to supply and demand as far as the prices of those stocks are concerned. Thus, if there is more 'demand' for a stock, then the price will increase, while if there is less 'demand' and more 'supply', the price will decrease.

The most common method to purchase stocks is through a brokerage. There are two different types of brokerage. The full-service brokerage charges a lot for offering you expert advice, and even for managing your account. On the other hand, discount brokerages offer a lot less as far as personal attention is concerned, but they are really much cheaper. These are the online discount brokers and thanks to them, it is easy for almost everyone out there to invest in the stock market.

It is impossible to close this chapter without discussing what the 'bulls and bears' are all about. It is not half as dicey as explaining the 'birds and bees' to your teenage child, though. Let us take a look at what these terms, that you will hear every now and then, whilst in the process of stock trading, really mean.

Bullish market

A 'bull' market is one in which everything seems to be going just great; the economy is superlative, GDP is rising and people are getting jobs. Of course, it is easier to pick up your stocks in this kind of market because everything is really going 'up'. A person who is optimistic and feels that the stock price will only go 'up', is called a 'bull'. Of course, the drawback is that a bull market cannot last forever and sometimes the stock prices get overvalued.

A bullish market is better known as an investor's market. The bullish market is quite ideal as the prices of stocks will be on a steady rise. This makes it a lucrative opportunity for investors to invest money in the market.

The term bullish comes from the word bull. Just like how the bull raises its horns in the air to attack its prey, the market lifts up the stocks and flings them in the air. The bullish market is every investor's dream market.

But remember, even if a bullish market exists, it does not guarantee that every kind of stock will remain bullish. Some stocks are not affected by the overall market conditions and will follow a course that they have etched for themselves.

Bearish market

A bear market is just the opposite of the 'Bull' market. This is when a recession has kicked in and investors are finding it hard to pick stocks. People either 'short sell' in this case to make money, or wait the 'bearish' period, and then start to buy in anticipation of the stocks going up. A person, who is pessimistic and thinks that the stocks are going to fall, is called a 'bear'.

A bearish market is the opposite of a bullish market. A bearish market is the one where all the prices of stocks are falling. So, it is better known as a seller's market, as people will prefer to sell out the stocks for the fear of losing money.

The bearish market is dreaded by most investors, as it would be risky to make any investment at such time. However, contrarians would not mind the risk and would be eager to buy stocks in time.

The term bearish comes from the word bear. Just like how a bear swoops down to attack its prey, the market swoops down on the stocks.

Bullish bar reversal

The bullish bar reversal is the one where the lowest days are lower than the previous day's low and the current price is higher than the previous day's high. As soon as this happens, the situation is called a bullish bar reversal. This type is ideal for a stock, as its price pattern will begin to reverse, which means that it will start getting better for the stock. Investors rejoice when such a pattern occurs.

Bearish bar reversal

Bearish bar reversal is the opposite of the bullish bar reversal. Such a situation arises when today's current price is lower than yesterday's closing price. This means that the price of the stock is on a downward trend. This can be because of many reasons and it is best to wait this period out rather than making hasty decisions.

What is the Market to Day Trade?

There are three different markets for day trading. They are forex, futures, and stock market. Most people are aware of the stock market but, not future and forex.

Stock Market: When people think of day trading, stock market comes into their mind first. It is best considered when it comes to buying and selling company shares. Therefore you will need to exit all positions by the end of the trading period. There is a requirement to hold at least $25k in your account, anything less will not be accepted in day trading. The required capital to start is $30k.

Future Market: This is another market for day trading. This is where there is an agreement between a seller and a buyer. They agree to sell or buy at an agreed amount, at a certain time. Traders make their gains from price fluctuations. This is from the difference computed between what is bought or what is sold and when the position closes. For this market, you do not need too much capital, a minimum of $3500, and a maximum of $5k is enough to start. The opening hours vary, you need to be careful and ensure that before the trade closes, you are out. You need to consider access to the future market and know the requirements. Usually, there is a limit on the minimum balance; it is set at $2k.

Forex Market: This is considered a common and accessible market; it trades for 24 hours in a day. The traders are allowed to start with a minimum capital of around $100 but it is mainly recommended to start with at least $500. They only deal with one currency and that could be a limitation when it comes to the investment currency. There are also specifications and requirements for this trading platform. As a trader, you need to be careful of the platform that you choose, ensure it is something that fits your preferences and needs.

There are demo accounts that can be used to practice and apply the techniques you have learned.

Several factors will affect your choice for a trading market. They include your financial position, the trading technique, interests, and personality. An example is when you want to start trading and your capital is below $25k. You will not be able to trade unless you continue saving up. When your capital is adequate, you can choose any of the trading markets listed above. You need to know that other techniques will work in one market and not the other.

And others will work at a certain time and others not. When you decide to adopt a technique, choose one market, and stick to that one. When you are new to day trading, do not flip between markets, but maintain a market. You are allowed to shift between trades based on the time you are trading.

All three markets are considered great. You will choose a market based on your preference and interest. However, it is recommended to stick to one market, as you know more about the others.

Chapter 5

What is Best to Trade?

When it comes to buying and selling stocks, it is entirely up to the investor to choose whatever he or she thinks will be a good investment. It is tough to generalize the type of stock that will suit everyone, as no one stock fits all rule. However, here are the types of stocks that you can deal with, in the share market.

Company Stocks

Company stocks are those that are issued by the company to their employees and also to the public. Although, top companies do not directly open up their shares for the public. Therefore, employees who own the shares can sell them in the market. There are several multinational companies to choose from including Microsoft, Coca Cola, Intel, Apple Inc., Nokia etc. You can choose a company that you think will help you increase the value of your investment. You will have to research the companies which are doing well and which ones are not, and choose to invest in them accordingly. But do not be in too much of a hurry to find the best stocks for you. Take your time and observe the trend for a few months. Once you establish a pattern, you can start buying the stocks of that company.

Commodities

The commodities market is where several types of commodities are bought and sold. These commodities can be of the following types:

Agricultural

Agricultural commodities are food items such as vegetables, fruits, pulses, and other crops. Each commodity has a different price and depending on which crops are doing well, you can decide to invest in them. These commodities are ideal for day trading as they generally rise in value by the end of the day. Some of the most preferred commodities include potatoes, pulses, rice, and sugar.

Metal

Metals are also a good market for investors. Metals such as copper, nickel, iron, and lead all have a good market value. It is possible for you to trade in these metals and you will have to look for the ones that are doing well currently. You can choose to hold on to them for a specific period of time and then sell them before the deal's expiry date.

Industrial

Industrial solvents, chemicals, and other such liquid commodities are also quite popular. They are in constant demand and command high prices. You can choose the ones that you think will fetch you a good price and invest in them.

Energy

Energy resources such as crude oil, petroleum, paraffin, etc. are also traded. These are required to fuel your cars, used in cosmetics, etc. and so, are in constant demand. You can choose the one that you think is in good demand and trade with them.

Livestock

Just like the other commodities, livestock is also traded on a daily basis in the stock market. These include pigs, sheep, etc. Many factors can affect their prices including weather conditions, diseases, and also their market demand and supply.

These form the various types of commodities that you can choose from, and you can purchase one type or diversify, by purchasing several types.

Currencies

When it comes to day trading, it is possible for the investor to trade in currencies. As an investor, you have a lot of choices and flexibility to hedge your currency exposure to risk. FX options, as currency trading in the options markets, is popularly known as, to allow the same core hedging and trading strategies used when trading options on ETFs, stocks, and indexes. The best and most straightforward way to remember what type of "option" you need to trade on, is to focus on the base currency or the first currency in every currency pair. The second currency in the pair is the quote currency or the counter currency. "Options" prices are typically derived from the base currency and are relative to the quote currency.

A USD-based currency pair (per USD) is available for the ten FX pairs. For instance, when you expect the US dollar to strengthen against the Japanese yen, you purchase YUK calls. In the inverse situation, when you expect the yen to strengthen against the US dollar, you purchase YUK puts.

It is up to you to decide what you think is best suited to trade with, depending on the resources you have at hand. You do not need to have extensive knowledge of these products, just only a little knowledge is enough for you to know if the products are worth investing in.

Index

Index trading refers to a type of trading where you bet on the index's rise and fall. Each sector of the stock exchange will have an index, which will take into account the prices of all the stocks that are listed under that index. Then by dividing it by the number of stocks present in the market, you will get a certain number. All of these indexes are pooled and a final index is prepared which is the entire share market's collective index. Now you can "bet" on where the index will reach by the end of the day. For this reason, you must study the individual indexes such as the IT industry index, the consumer goods index, etc. Once you think you know where the index will be by the end of the day, you can invest in it.

ETF

An ETF is also known as Exchange Traded Funds. These ETF's are like mini mutual funds that are traded in the market. Each ETF will have a combination of different underlying securities and these will be split into several small pieces. You can buy these in bulk and they can be traded on a daily basis. The main idea is to buy them at a low price and then dispose of them at a higher price. You have to understand that they are slow movers and you will have to buy them, and consequently wait for them to grow in value. These are much preferred as they will give you the advantage of a mutual fund but can be exchanged daily.

Bonds

Bonds are securities that are issued by companies and can be bought and sold to realize a profit. These bonds can come in several different forms and are explained below:

Government bonds

Government bonds refer to those bonds that are issued by the government. As you may know, the government requires funds from time to time and will ask you to pay forward. Once you do that, they will issue you a bond that is valued much lower than its actual value. After it matures, you can collect the amount you paid along with the interest that they would pay you. If at any time you wish to sell the bond, then you can do so and you will get paid a higher amount for it. The government might also agree to pay you a certain percentage interest every month and you can capitalize on this opportunity to keep your money safe and also earn a profit from it. This form of investment is extremely safe as the government will not default on paying you your due money.

Agency bonds

Agency bonds are much like government bonds. They are run by companies that the government funds. So these can be counted as government bonds. They will pay you a great rate of interest on your investment. However, you cannot expect the same guarantee from them, as you would from the government bonds. You might have to invest a certain fixed sum as well. But given their success rate, they are a great option for all of those who are looking to safeguard their money and, also earn a certain rate of return on it. The same rules apply to agency bonds when you wish to liquidate them. You can sell them at a higher price or collect your sum and interest at the time of maturity.

Federal bonds

Your local governments issue federal bonds. Just like how the central government issues bonds, your local governments will do the same. You can buy these bonds at low rates, and then hold on to them. You can sell them whenever you like, and earn a higher income from it. These bonds will pay you more than what your government bonds will, as your local government will not need a lot of money for a high scale project and, it will be slightly low key. This type of investment will be much better than saving in the bank, which will pay you much less interest.

Corporate bonds

Corporate bonds refer to those that are issued by companies. As you know, multinational companies also require money for their projects. This money will raise by issuing bonds to the public. They will agree to pay you back after a while, and until then, they will pay you a fixed rate of interest. You can sell these bonds for a profit at any time. But you must understand that these companies will not provide you with a guarantee, just like your government and federal government bonds would do. So, this is a risk that you will be taking. However, if you choose a big multinational company, then you might hit a jackpot. Not only will you get paid more, but also win over their loyalty. They might be willing to give you shares in their company at a discounted rate, which will be a bonus for you. You can then sell these stocks at a later date, and realize a big profit from it!

Zero coupon bonds

Zero-coupon bonds are extremely popular owing to their ease of trade. They are extremely liquid and there is always a high request for them. Now, suppose a zero-coupon bond is worth $500, when you buy it, they will issue it at $100, and ask you to exchange it for $500 in 2 years. So despite it being valued at $100 now, you will get back 4 times the value after exchanging it at the expiry of 2 years. So, not only your money will be safe, but you will also be able to increase its value several-fold.

Chapter 6

Trading Basic Concepts

How Day Trading Works

Understanding how day trading works is pretty easy and straightforward. First and foremost, we have day traders, active traders, and even hyperactive day traders. Terms depend on the number of trades entered per day and even per year.

To be profitable, a day trader counts on volatility. Volatility refers to the abrupt rise, and fall in the price of securities such as shares and currencies. Day traders love stocks that experience a lot of volatility and move a lot in the course of the trading day. However, stocks do not just move for no reason. There are certain causes of market volatility. Some of these include company news, the state of the general economy, investor sentiments, earnings reports, and so on.

Apart from volatility, day traders also prefer highly liquid stocks. This means, that a trader is easily able to enter and exit trades when the stocks are liquid. They can also exit without altering the stock price by any significant margin.

Individual and Corporate Day Traders

There are generally two types of day traders. We have day traders who are independent and earn their living through day trading. We also have day traders, who work for corporations. These, constitute the majority of day traders. They enjoy certain benefits of working together in large groups, compared to individual retail traders.

One of the benefits that corporate day traders enjoy, is access to large amounts of capital. They also enjoy plenty of leverage that enables them to enter numerous traders and exit profitably. They even have a direct line as well as a trading desk. These, are facilities that other traders would die to have. They also enjoy access to superior analytical software and unlimited funds.

For these reasons, they can take on more trades and trade with lots of leverage. They are also able to enter positions that other traders cannot. Corporate day traders find arbitrage opportunities to make easy profits throughout the trading day. They mostly focus on easy trades that are less risky way before the other traders move in. With the resources that they have as well as the opportunities presented by the markets, day traders are able to trade successfully and generate lots of profits.

Some day traders, either use their own money or use other people's money to trade. However, most day traders previously worked for corporations and, as such have access to certain beneficial facilities like a trading desk. A lot of them have relationships with brokerage firms, as they spend lots of funds paying commissions. However, individual retail traders are not in a position to compete fairly with institutional traders.

They lack the facilities, and financial resources needed to engage in large-scale, profitable trades like their corporate counterparts. This is the reason why such traders often take on riskier trades, just so they can make sufficient profits.

Day trading is not something that you should take for granted. You have to ask yourself if you want to get involved or not. There are some things that you should consider having before you become a day trader, and that is why we are here for you, giving a hand on understanding day trading strategies.

Before you jump into the world of day trading, you must amass some knowledge concerning the world of trading. You have to find out your level of risk tolerance, goals, as well as capital.

Day trading is a career that you have to invest time into. If you have decided to try it out, you have to spend time practicing it before you start live trading. As you practice, you improve your strategies. Only then, you can use real money to try it out? You need al of this practice to invest your time. Day trading is not something that can be done successfully, just for the urge to do it. You must spend your time and energy into it if you want to succeed.

If you have decided that trading is something that you want to consider, you should think of starting up as little as possible. Go for a few stocks or currencies initially, instead of trying to enter the market with a boom, because at the end of the day you will thin yourself out. If you go all out initially, you will end up confusing yourself, and this could lead to a large number of losses.

You should be calm while you trade. Shut off your emotions while you trade. Use only facts and do not try to make use of emotions because they could mislead you.

The more you can take out the emotional aspect, the more you can be faithful to the plan that you have laid out. When you are calm, it permits you to be focused.

Chapter 7

Average Income of a Day Trader

Imagine a scenario where I reveal to you that exchanging salary has numerous factors, by applying some essential research strategies. You can go to a reliable gauge of what an informal investor can make, depending on their area, beginning capital, and business status.

In this section, I will share with you, various sources that give you clear gauges, so that you can be able to use and decide your potential benefit.

Let us face it, a significant number of people are thinking about going out without anyone else and, are not hoping to find a new line of work.

Anybody that discloses to you a conclusive range for a day exchanging pay, is likely pulling your leg.

Presently, for all you corporate individuals that can converse with your insider companions to check the amount you can make in an exchanging work, kindly do not anticipate hard numbers from any of these sources.

The reason being, there is a large group of outside variables that play into how a lot of cash you can make. In this article, we will tear through all the lighting on the web and get down to cold hard certainties. Sit back, unwind, and get some espresso.

A Decision You Should Not Take Lightly

You ought not to trifle with this choice, and you should gauge the upsides and downsides. First of all, exchanging for another person will permit you the chance to use the devices and systems of an outfit that is ideally beneficial.

A portion of the positives of exchanging for another person is evacuating the weights of distinguishing both a triumphant framework and a tutor that can help you en route.

If you are not beneficial "enough," be set up to have a more significant number of rules tossed at you, then when you were in sixth grade.

This degree of administration over your exchanging action, is because of the reality you are utilizing another person's cash, to profit or become acclimated to somebody revealing to you, how to relax.

The one significant upside for day exchanging for another person is that you will get paid. This pay is likely insufficient to live on, however, you do get a check.

At the point that you decide to go on your own, there is no pay. You are a financial specialist wanting to make payments. We will discuss this theme further on. However, I needed to ensure I express this forthright.

Licenses

On the slim chance that you choose to work for the firm, and are exchanging customer's cash or conceivably interfacing with clients, you will require your Series 7 and perhaps your Series 63 permit.

Arrangement 7

The Series 7 will give you the permit to exchange. Last I checked, the test cost $305 and relying upon the outfit will be secured by the firm.

Arrangement 63

The Series 63 is the test that you should take after Series 7. This test licenses you to request orders for stock, depending on the point of view of the state.

A straightforward perspective about this is the 7 that gives you the privilege to exchange on a government level, and the 63 enables you to work inside the limits of state laws.

I will not anticipate covering the theme of day exchanging for somebody finally, because I have not lived it.

From what I do know, you are required to finish some in-house preparing programs for the firm you speak to. For venture houses, you will get a not too bad base pay, enough to keep you at the lower white-collar class, extend for New York.

Need to know the best part?

Your base stock merchant pay could go from 50,000 to 70,000 dollars US, which is only enough for you to take care of your link tab, feed yourself, and perhaps take a taxi or two. In any case, this is not the slightest bit covers meals, vehicles, excursions, tuition-based schools, and so on.

In this way, I surmise that you can rapidly observe that for you to be fruitful, you are going to need to make your reward. There is only one catch, you need to profit day exchanging.

Superficially, this sounds sensible because you bring down your hazard profile by having another pay stream of base compensation. In any case, you need to perform to remain utilized, and will just get around 10-30% of the benefits that you get from your exchanging movement.

In light of these numbers, you would need to make about 300k in exchanging benefits to break a 100k in compensation.

Most likely about it, the advantage of exchanging with an organization is, after some time, your purchasing influence will increment, and you have none of the drawbacks dangers since it is the organization's cash. The key is ensuring you have a lot of money under administration.

As it should be evident in the finished infographic, the way for making genuine cash, is to begin dealing with different assets. You, in one way or another, draw that off, and you will make by a large 576k per year.

Indeed, you read that right.

I realize the 576k looks engaging; however, remember, it is difficult and hard labor to get to the highest point of the mountain.

The other thing that brings up to get out from the infographic, is that the usual reward is beginning to drift higher, and if things go as conjecture, it will surpass the downturn top not long from now.

Along these lines, on the off possibility that one of your objectives is to profit, you are looking at the right business.

Regular Income Trading for a Company

The widely appealing individual can hope to make somewhere in the range of 100k and 175k. In conclusion, it is on the off chance that you are beneath normal.

In any case, there is more.

Certainly, if we broaden our exploration past New York, you will see that the regular pay for a "Merchant" is $89,496.

Try not to trust me!

Open Trading Firms

Be that as it may, I can consider many employments where you can make near $89k, which do not require the degree of responsibility and hazard taking required for exchanging.

You might be thinking, "this person just revealed to me that the earnings could go as high as $250k to $500k, in case I'm better than expected, where does $89k become an integral factor."

What I have talked about so far, are the pay rates traded on an open market organization.

Good karma attempting to get precise information for the first-class universe of private value brokers. What you will discover, is regularly the top brokers from the Chase and Bank of America's endeavor out to flexible investments, as a result of the opportunity in their exchanging choices, and the more significant potential compensation.

Here is the most significant part, with the general population firms, corporate objectives will frequently drive a segment of your other targets.

The magnificence of the multifaceted investment world is, while there are still organization objectives, you have the chance to get a more significant amount of what you work for.

It is nothing for a top broker to out-acquire their chief on the off chance, that they carry enough an incentive to the firm.

What amount do you figure you could make?

Advantages of day exchanging for an organization

1. Pay
2. Medical advantages
3. The renown of working for a venture bank or fence investments
4. No danger of individual capital
5. Climb the corporate positions to deal with various assets
6. A drawback of day exchanging for an organization
7. Must connect with customers
8. Office legislative issues
9. By and large, you get 20% of benefits (Public Firm)

Day Trading for a Prop Firm

Day exchanging for prop firms can feel similar in living on the edge.

Like exchanging for an organization, you will get some preparation before the prop firm enables you to trade with their cash, and approach their frameworks. From that point forward, all likenesses between exchanging for a prop firm, and an organization contrast.

Try not to expect any human services paid downtime. You will not have a base compensation or yearly audits. The prop firms will expect you to store cash to begin utilizing their foundation.

The advantages are that the prop firm will part benefits with you anyplace from a third, and up to half. The drawbacks are again no compensation, and you bear a portion of the torment with regards to misfortunes.

However, here is the rub, the explanation prop firm merchants make not precisely those for the speculation houses, is access to capital. Since you are likely exchanging the exclusive firm proprietor's cash, the pool of assets you approach is constrained.

I would state better than an expected broker for a prop firm can make about 150k to 250k every year. The typical broker will do somewhere in the range of 60k and 100k, and underperformers will have such huge numbers of position limits set for them, they are fundamentally rehearsing, and not profiting. These underperformers will probably expel themselves from the game because rehearsing does not take care of the tabs.

Advantages
- Split benefits with Prop Firm
- Low commission rates
- No Boss
- Increment Margin

Negatives
- Utilize your cash-flow to begin
- Loss of individual riches
- Constrained preparing
- No medical advantages or paid downtime
- No vocation movement
- Just cause cash off what you to acquire

Day Trading Salaries State by State in the US

Notwithstanding the information showed in the infographic from the Office of the New York State Comptroller, I needed to make it a stride further to distinguish the beginning pay for a passage level exchanging work over the country.

Now, I am arriving at a passage level to give a counter to the middle national normal of $89k for an exchanging work. Keep in mind that $89k is normal for a junior exchanging employments - right to the most senior.

Along these lines, in the situation that you are genuinely beginning and are offered $50k, would you not want to be in another place?

True to form, the New England and Pacific districts of the nation, have the most significant pay. Presently, these can be just ascribed to the standard average cost of essential items. However, you can discover your state to perceive what you can hope to make as a lesser dealer.

The Myth

A large number of the online articles are explicit about the benefit proportion you can expect when you become an informal investor. For instance, an article by Cory Mitchell that shows up on the Vantage Point Trading site spreads it out in detail, and expect to start exchanging capital of $30,000:

"Accept your five normal exchanges for every day, so if you have 20 exchanging days a month, you make 100 exchanges for every month. You make $3,750, however, despite everything, you have commissions and perhaps some different charges. Your expense per exchange is $5/contract (full circle). Your bonus costs are: 100 exchanges x $5 x 2 agreements = $1000."

In Mitchell's model, your net after bonuses is $2,750. Since you began with $30,000, that is a month to month return of a little more than 9 percent. If you reinvest those benefits on a month to month premise, toward the end of one year, you will have an interest of $55,944 and change. Not awful, and the best news is, you do not have to get dressed for work.

The Reality

Here is a sure sign that the truth might not be very quite the same as the legend.

As indicated by a 2013 investigation of the Taiwanese securities exchange drove by business analyst Brad Barber of the University of California, Davis, Graduate School of Management, and including the ordinary trade that market over 14 years, under 1 percent of all member dealers made a benefit. Putting it another way, 99 percent of throughout the informal investors lost cash.

Another concentrates by Barber and individual UC financial analyst Terrance Odean dissected the market returns of more than 66,000 U.S. families exchanging the U.S. securities exchange over a five-year time frame from 1991 to 1996. They reasoned that continuous dealers (not informal investors, mainly, however, including casual investors and the individuals who exchange stocks as often as possible) failed to meet expectations financial specialists who utilized a purchase and hold methodology by about a third. The more as often as possible a given member exchanged, the more they failed to meet expectations the average return.

Genuine later consider, similar to the 2013 research learn at the Cass Business School at the City University of London, reasoned that dealers tossing darts at the stock pages could accomplish preferable outcomes over stock merchants. All right, they have carefully reenacted dealers, yet at the same time.

To give you a superior thought of your odds as a "proficient" informal investor, think about that the administrative North American Securities Administrators Association records exchanging courses – the web-based "exchanging schools", that idea, to show you how to prevail as an informal investor – as a best 10 risk to financial specialists, alongside Ponzi, plans and obscure exchanging calculations depend on Fibonacci numbers.

A Day Trading Strategy in real life

Accept a day exchanging system where the stop misfortune is $0.04, and your objective is $0.06.

Your record balance is $30,000, so the most hazard per exchange is $300. With a $0.04 stop misfortune, you can take 7,500 ($300/$0.04) shares on each trade and remain in your $300 chance top (excluding commissions).

If it is not too much issue, take note that to receive 7,500 offers, the offer cost should be underneath $16 (achieved by $120,000 in purchasing power isolated by 7,500 proposals) if the per-share price is more than $16 you will have to take fewer offers. The stock additionally needs to have enough volume for you to make such a position (see Look for These Qualities in a Day Trading Stock).

Working with this procedure, here is an example of the amount you might make by day exchanging stocks:

55 exchanges were victors/gainful: 55 x $0.06 x 7,500 shares = $24,750

45 exchanges were failures: 45 x - $0.04 x 7500 shares = ($13,500)

Your gross benefit would be $24,750 - $13,500 = $11,250.

Your net benefit, which incorporates the expense of commissions, is $11,250 - commissions ($30 x 100 = $3,000) = $8,250 for the month.

This is the hypothetical benefit, and a few elements can and will lessen your interests; see Refinements beneath to perceive how this number gets balanced for this present reality.

The reward chance proportion of 1.5 is used because, it is genuinely traditionalist and intelligent for the open doors that happen throughout the day, consistently in the financial exchange.

The beginning capital of $30,000 is additionally a surmised equalization to begin day exchanging stocks; more is prescribed on the off chance that you wish to trade more costly stocks.

The $0.04 stop and $0.06 are utilized similarly, for instance. Contingent upon the unpredictability of the stock, this may be diminished, yet more than likely extended if the stock moves a ton. As the stop continues, you will have to lessen the number of offers taken to keep up a similar degree of hazard insurance.

Refinements to Your Strategy

Frequently on winning exchanges, it will not be conceivable to get every one of the offers you need; the value moves too rapidly. In this way, accept for winning exchanges you end up with, by and large, 6,000 offers. This diminishes the net benefit to $3,300, rather than $8,250.

Little modifications can affect gainfulness.

Some different presumptions were likewise made in the model above. Chiefly that the dealer can locate a stock that enables them to ultimately use their capital (counting influence) while utilizing a 1.5 reward-to-hazard proportion, discovering five exchanges a day will be more troublesome on certain days than others (perceive How to Find Volatile Stocks for Day Trading).

Value slippage is additionally a particular piece of exchanging. That is the point at which a more significant misfortune happens than anticipated, in any event, when utilizing a stop misfortune. Slippage will, to a great extent, rely upon the volume of the stock compared with your position size.

To represent slippage, decrease your net gain figures at any 10 % rate. Given this situation and refinements, it is conceivable to make about $2,970, exchanging a $30,000 account (the $3,300 referenced above, diminished by 10 %).

Modify this situation in a like manner dependent on your stop and target (standard reward to chance), capital, slippage, win rate, standard wins/misfortune position sizes, and commissions. Given your proposed methodology, it is conceivable to inquire about quite a bit of this before you start exchanging to get a thought of the amount you can make.

The amount Money Stock Day Traders Make - Final Word

The above situation shows that it is conceivable to make more than 20% for each month with daily exchanges, hypothetically. This is high by regular measures and most brokers should not hope to do this when they pose exact problems. For example, slip and not continually get a chance to get the full position they want on winning trades.

With a 55% payout rate and a procedure that produces winners more significant than bankruptcies, going from 5% to 15%, every month is conceivable. However, it is not easy, even if the numbers make it seem so. These figures speak of what is feasible for those who become fruitful in the course of daytime exchanges; remember, however, the exchange of days has a low rate of results, particularly among boys.

Chapter 8

Trading Strategies and Techniques

When it comes to trading, there are more strategies available than I can possibly put in one book. Part of the reason for this is because so many strategies can be used for different types of trading and investing. Another reason is that traders seem to be coming up with new forms of techniques all the time. However, I have chosen some of the most popular strategies that are used by day traders to outline here.

ABCD Pattern

This is a strategy that uses a specific pattern in order to help you find the exact time you should sell your stock. There are four parts to this pattern:

A - the initial high price of the stock.

B - the lowest price of the stock, which occurs when people start selling once they see the stock has hit A.

C - the establishment of the higher low. This is the point where people who follow the ABCD pattern will start the selling process of their stock.

D - the highest profitable point. This is the point the stock rises to, which gives the day trader a large profit.

This strategy is known to not only be a bit tricky but also risky. This is because the trader has to sell at the specified point of C, which is when the stock starts to rise in price after reaching point B. Of course, the biggest risk is that the stock falls below point B after the trader sells at point C. This would mean that the trader receives a bigger loss than anyone who sold right after point A. However, the hope is that the price of the stock rises past point A, which gives the trader a large profit.

The ABCD pattern I explained above is just one of the patterns that you will see as a trader. Some patterns show point A to be the lowest price and point B to be the stock's highest price. However, the trader still sells at point C and hopes to reach point D to gain the best profit.

Bull Flag Momentum

This strategy received its bull flag name because the trend lines resemble a flagpole. After the stock reaches a high price, it has a short-term downtrend. However, it quickly spikes up before spiking back down another time. This trend tends to repeat itself once again and leaves a model in which high and low prices are parallel to each other. However, the pattern ends when the price spikes back up, exceeding the previous highest price. This is when traders begin to sell and hope to make the best profit.

The trick to catching the bull flag strategy is that you look for the pattern where the high and low prices are parallel to each other, yet they are either slowly moving up or down the chart. Both of these directions signal that the stock can quickly spike up in price and exceed its previous high price.

Volume Weighted Average Price (VWAP) Trading

VWAP trading takes the price and volume of stock to give you an average price. It is known as a trading benchmark which will give to traders an idea of the trend and the security of the stock. Like most trading strategies, the VWAP can be used with specific software that will perform the algorithms for each step. However, it is possible to calculate the VWAP by yourself.

This type of strategy can be used by various investors and traders. For example, both day traders and buy-and-hold investors can use the VWAP technique. However, it is more popular with short-term trades. This kind of strategy will start new every beginning of the day and will give you a running total at the end of the day. This is one of the reasons why buy-and-hold investors use this strategy, as it allows them to analyze the stock.

Electronic Communication Network (ECN) and Level II

This type of strategy involves watching the trades in real-time. It is similar to going to a horse race and watching the race to see if you are going to win or lose your money. The ECN is an automated system where traders from all over the world can trade with you. Day traders who take on the business by themselves, without the help of a broker, usually use the ECN strategy because it is fairly easy to navigate and is known to take out any middleman. This is a benefit as it takes away any brokerage fees and can make trades more profitable because it is known to save time. On top of this, the ECN allows for after-market trading, which means you can trade after the regular trading hours of the day.

There are several charts available that will allow you to see the price changes of stocks throughout the day. All of the charts will allow you to compare the opening price up to the closing price. On top of this, the charts will also allow you to see the various price changes in the stock during the day.

1. Candlestick Charts

Most day traders use candlestick charts as they find them essential for the business. These charts are helpful because they will display specific security prices on a daily basis. Once you learn how to analyze candlestick charts, you will be able to tell when the highest and lowest prices for any of your stocks will be, which will help you increase your profits. Furthermore, you will be able to learn where the stock sits at both opening and closing that day. If the candlestick has a red or black color, then the closing price of the stock is lower than the opening price. If the candlestick has a green or white color, then you know that the closing price is higher than the opening price. You can also analyze more about the stock through the shadow of the candlestick. The shadow will tell you what the prices were throughout the stock's day. You can then take this analysis and compare it to the opening and closing prices.

2. Line Charts

Line charts are another popular chart type that day traders use often. While these charts give you the same information as candlestick charts, they will only work if you have the specified charting software. However, this is becoming more typical with any type of chart you want to use. This is because the charting software that is on the market today will allow you to develop the charts you want to use and include all the information you need in order to analyze the stocks on a daily basis.

3. Bar Charts

Many day traders like to use bar charts because some of them are definitely easier to read. There are four main prices that you will find if you use bar charts. The first one is the opening price. The second one is the highest price and the third one is the lowest price of the day. The final price you will see through the chart is the closing price. Through these four prices, you can start to analyze what the day-to-day process is for any stock you are interested in.

Spread Trading

Spread trading, also known as scalping, is defined as trading securities over a period of seconds to minutes. The reason this type of technique has become popular is because traders feel that they can catch stocks easier when they follow small growths over large increments. The number of transactions day traders go through can vary from a dozen to over 200 within a day. Traders make so many transactions because they will sell the stock as soon as possible since it will give them a profit.

This type of technique is known to be relatively safe, which is another reason why so many traders consider themselves spread traders. Traders who follow this technique are often considered to be market makers, as they help maintain the liquidity of the market.

If you are thinking about looking more into this strategy, then you will want to note the following three points:

- Low Profits Comes from Large Volume

Traders who use the spread trading technique state this strategy is not useful for people who want to move large volumes of shares at one time. They will not be able to make the money they want by using this strategy as large volumes give low profits. This happens because the profit margin, which is the measure of profitability, neglects the large volume investor. Therefore, the best type of traders for spread trading are those people who are interested in moving small volumes.

- You Will Have a Lower Risk if You Lower Your Exposure

Traders who take on the technique of scalping will limit their risk of loss because they do not hang onto their stocks for a long period of time. In fact, most traders will hold on to the majority of their shares for only a few minutes, very rarely reaching an hour.

- Smaller Moves are Easier

I have already stated that you would want to move small volumes in order to gain the best benefits as a spread trader. People who follow this technique become pros at finding the small moves with the small spreads that tend to happen frequently throughout the day. The reason spread traders focus on small moves is not only because they are easier to handle using this technique but also because this is where they will find their best profits.

Trend Following

Traders refer to trend following as trading stocks because of their trends over their market value. This type of technique is not only used in day trading, but in all types of stock market transactions. How long you will follow the trend before you decide to take a stock because of its trend depends on what type of trading you are doing. In day trading, you will not spend more than a couple of hours on the trend. However, if you are into swing trading, you might analyze the trend for a few days to a couple of weeks.

Many traders like to take part in this technique because they feel that they know what the stock is going to do. Because you have watched for a trend to develop and then analyzed the trend to make sure it is a purchase you would like to make, your confidence about what the stock will do in the future increases. On top of this, many traders feel that they are more likely to succeed in making a profit because they can watch for stocks that will give you capital instead of a loss.

At the same time, you always want to pay attention to all the factors that affect the trend of a stock. The factors you should consider if you decide to use trend following are:

- Money Management

Money management is one consideration as if you have too much money, then you are risking losing more money than you should. However, if you do not have enough money, you are unlikely to reap the benefits of that trade. When you look at money management, you pay a lot of attention to your risk, which will let you know how much money you should put into that stock.

Price

The most important factor you will want to pay attention to is the price of the stock. While day traders pay attention to price variations of the stock, the most important price to look at is the actual price of the stock at the moment. It is the actual price that will tell you whether you should invest in the stock or hold off.

Diversity

Diversity is a word that you will often see in the stock market. This refers to the different types of stocks that you have in your portfolio. This is also a term that you will find some traders following while some traders feel it is a waste of time. While it is controversial, there are many benefits of diversity, especially for traders and serious investors. On top of this, when you use diversity, you are able to follow trends better, as it is an important factor of trend following.

Risk

Another factor to consider is the amount of risk that comes with the trend. While you can never get rid of *all* the risks in trading, you want to limit it as much as possible. If you find you are looking at a trend that is high in risk, you may want to pick a different stock, especially as a day trader. However, there are traders who like stocks with higher risk. How much risk you are willing to take on in a stock is a personal preference. However, most experienced day traders say that if you truly want to be successful, you will limit your risk as much as possible.

Rules

Finally, you will always want to follow the rules. Not only follow the rules of day trading, but you will also want to follow the rules you have created for yourself. One reason for this is that it helps you remain consistent in your trading, which will help increase your success rate. Another reason is that your rules will help you become systematic when you are choosing your stocks.

News Playing

This is a technique that day traders use when they follow the news of the stock market. When most people think of the stock market, they imagine a person reading the newspaper to see how the price of stocks is doing that day. This is similar to the news playing, however, most day traders pay attention to several sources of information. You can get the news information from any online communities you join, news outlets, or any other reports which are easily found online.

One of the most important factors when following the news playing technique is to make sure you keep your emotions in check. Experienced traders know well how emotions can affect your decisions when trading. They also know how this can cause a trader to lose a lot of money. One of the most popular historic examples of how emotions can affect the stock market is the stock market crash of 1929. This is the event that helped launch the United States into the Great Depression, which lasted throughout the 1930s. One of the reasons the crash occurred was because of all the investors who decided to quickly sell their stocks because they saw the prices dropping. They started to get anxious over the money they would lose if they did not sell. On top of that, they started to worry about the stock market in general because the prices were becoming so low. Emotions were running high on Wall Street right before the stock market crash, which did not help the situation at all. In fact, many historians state that if people would have kept their stocks instead of selling them, America would have never seen such a horrible depression in its economy. As stated before, when stocks sell, the price declines. Therefore, the more people who sell, the more the price will drop. Because the price of stocks kept dropping, more people started to sell. Eventually, this led to the stock market crash.

It is always a good thing to make sure you are thinking logically when you are making decisions in the stock market. If you find yourself thinking illogically, you are putting too much emotion into your decision. One of the best things to do when this happens is simply to take a break or pick a stock that you do not feel too much emotion towards. It is also important to remember that day trading is not for everyone. If you are naturally a person with strong emotions, you might want to look at different trading or investing methods.

You also want to make sure that you continue to do your research. Once you see a news report, you want to look into how this news is affecting the stock. For example, if you read that CVS Pharmacy donated thousands of dollars to a struggling community, you might find their stock prices increasing. The news can easily affect who buys and sells a company's stocks, as investors want to purchase stocks from companies they believe will be successful and are proud to own a share of. Therefore, the price of the stock will go up, but the value might also increase.

Of course, there is always negative news which can also affect stocks. If you find that you hold a stock in a company and you see a negative news article about them, you will probably want to sell your stock as quickly as possible because this will allow you to sell with less loss.

Fading

Not a lot of traders take part in fading because it is known to be one of the riskier strategies. Unless you have a good amount of experience in trading, it is best that you do not participate in fading, as it is considered a more advanced technique in the business. The basis of short selling is that the trader speculates on the stock's decline. Speculation means that the trader makes the transaction when the risk of losing capital is high because the trader expects that there will be a benefit or some type of gain from the trade.

Fading does not follow the trends of the market. Traders buy when the price of the stock is low and sell when the price is high. They often buy a stock when they feel the market has overreacted over recent news. One of the benefits is that there is little analysis that needs to be done before buying or selling.

Stop-Loss Trading

This type of strategy involves making a deal with your broker to sell a stock once it reaches a certain price. This is a popular strategy, in fact, most experienced traders say you should use stop-loss trading because it gives you security in your business. This happens because you can decide to say that you will sell the stock when it is 13% below your purchasing price.

This type of strategy is not always used for day trading because sometimes the stock will not reach the percentage you set. Therefore, you continue to hold the stock and do not sell it at the end of the day.

Range Trading

Range trading is often compared to trend following, however they are different techniques. When you use range trading, you will watch a stock over a certain period of time. Like other techniques, the increase and decline of prices will present a pattern which is noticeable to the trader. The trader will watch the prices until they see a breakout in the pattern. A breakout is when the price dramatically inflates. The opposite of this, a breakdown, is when the price dramatically declines from its pattern. Once this happens, traders feel that this pattern will continue for some time.

In order to reduce risks when it comes to this strategy, traders will often set high and low limits. This means that once they have viewed where the stock's pattern is sitting for a couple of hours, they will set the highest and lowest price they will buy or sell. Then, once the breakout or breakdown occurs, the trader will take the step and buy or sell the stock.

Chapter 9

Investing Opportunities

There are many options for investing. Once the investor has determined the broker, and how much they would like to invest, it is time to determine what type of investment they wish to make. This is important to figure out before determining the specific stock that they wish to invest in. Different stocks serve different purposes; some may be highly beneficial for one investor to invest in while it may not be the best choice for another investor. It is important to determine the type of time period that the investor is wishing to invest in. For those interested in day trading or swing trading stocks, penny stocks and other speculative stocks may prove beneficial. On the other hand, dividend stocks may be beneficial for those utilizing the "buy and hold" method. The investor may wish to purchase stock the standard way or to use options. There is the option for forex stocks, as well. There are a variety of "funds," including trust funds, index funds, mutual funds, hedge funds, and ETFs. Investors should familiarize themselves with the differences between common and preferred stocks. There are also different types of orders that may be placed, which should also be differentiated by the investor. By familiarizing themselves with the different stock investment options, investors are helping to find the best choices for them in the investing world. It is crucial to learn about the different choices before jumping into any investments.

Trading Vs Buy And Hold

There are some traders that opt for a more long-term investment, choosing to buy the stock and hold onto it for a longer period. Others prefer a shorter-term investment, such as day trading or swing trading. Those that invest in the long-term have trades that last for months, years, and even decades. They buy it with the hope that it will increase over time. They may also hope to collect bonuses in the form of dividends. It is wisest to have a bit of both so that the investor can experience the benefits that both offer. This will also contribute to a more diversified portfolio. There are differences, however, in the requirements of both for the trader. Shorter-term trading requires more time and frequent research, while long-term investments are more of a source of passive income. Day traders typically spend at least a couple of hours each day studying the market and trading. Those who wish to invest in the long-term may research anytime, for as long as they wish. They may also wait as long as they would like to conduct any trades. These investors typically spend a couple of hours each month dedicated to trading. For day-trading stocks, there are usually minimum account balances to maintain, typically at least $25,000. This may completely vary based on the brokerage, yet the typical minimal fee for day-traders is higher than that of those wishing to invest in the long-term. Both require self-discipline. Short-term trading requires the trader to not act on their emotions and be patient with the amount of time that is required to dedicate to trading. Long-term traders must be patient with holding onto their investments for a long period of time.

There are two types of "shorter-term" investors: day traders and swing traders. Day traders conduct several trades a day based on analyses of the market. It takes great skill for a day trader to yield a high return on their investments. Swing traders, on the other hand, trade over the period of a few days, perhaps even a few weeks. It is a middle option between day trading and long-term investing. It takes less of a time commitment than day trading. Swing traders may experience both larger losses and gains than day traders due to the extended time period of the trade. They both require a time commitment and skills, yet day trading is a bit more demanding of the two.

While long-term investors may be on the lookout for stocks that offer dividends as well as long-term gain, short-term investors may be more likely to invest in penny stocks. These stocks are usually those of smaller companies and trade for under five dollars per share. They typically lack liquidity, as they usually trade infrequently. These are considered speculative stocks because there is a risk for the total or partial loss of the investment. Speculative stocks are stocks that the trader predicts will grow, despite a possible lack of evidence or history demonstrating such growth. Penny stocks are typically enjoyed by investors because more shares may be bought for a lower price. If there is adequate growth, this can prove highly profitable. However, investors frequently put a large amount of money into buying penny stocks because they are "cheaper" stocks. This can prove to be a high-risk trade.

Options Vs Stock

While stocks give you a portion of ownership in a company, options are contracts that give the owner the right to trade stocks at a particular price by a certain date. There are two types of options: puts and calls. The buyer of a call option has the right to purchase a stock at a set price before the expiration of the option. Those who buy a put option will have the right to sell a stock at a set price before the expiration of the option. The buyer or seller has the right to buy or sell options, but they are not obligated to do so. They own the asset until they sell it. When buying a call option, the investor has the right (but is not obligated) to buy the stock at a later date at a specific price. They are paying to pay for a later price. This may prove profitable if they agree to pay for a lower price, then the stock grows at that time. Call options are purchased when the investor believes that the stock price will increase in the next few months, whereas put options are purchased when the investor believes that the stock price will decrease over the next few months.

When one sells an option, they are writing that option, as options are created by individuals as opposed to companies. When one writes an option, they may be obligated to buy or sell that option before its expiration date. There are also two primary option styles: American and European. American-style options are more flexible, as they may typically be bought or sold at any time between the purchase date and date of expiration. European-style options may only be bought or sold on the expiration date. The price of an option is also known as its premium. The buyer of an option risks no more than the amount they paid for the option, as they cannot lose more than the initial premium paid. The seller, on the other hand, may lose more than the original premium, as they assume the risk of having to deliver or take delivery of the stock shares.

Options are typically available only in intervals ($0.50 or $1 for typical stocks, and $2.50 or $5 for higher-priced stocks).

All options have an expiration date. Normal options may expire up to nine months from the original list date. There are also long-term equity anticipation securities (LEAPS) available, which may allow for an expiration date of up to three years. The expiration date falls on a Friday (unless there is a holiday, in which case it will be moved back one business day).

The strike price is the price that the trader predicts that the stock will be above or below by the expiration date. A contract is the number of options that the trader will buy. One contract is one hundred shares of the stock. The premium is calculated by multiplying the call price by the number of contracts bought and multiplying that number by one hundred. This is the total amount paid for all contracts.

A call option that is "in the money" has a strike price lower than the current stock price, whereas a put option that is "in the money" has a strike price that is above the current stock price. A call option that is "out of the money" has a strike price higher than the current stock price, whereas a put option that is "out of the money" has a strike price that is below the current stock price.

Options Trading

Options trading is not the same as stock trading; these two kinds of trading are very different and hardly have similarities among themselves. One major difference between the two is that while stock trading gives shareholders' ownership rights in the form of dividends and voting power, options trading is just a mere paper contract that gives options holders the opportunity to buy and sell securities or stocks for a fixed price before a fixed date.

Options can be defined as a contract that gives an investor the option of buying or selling stocks or securities at a fixed price over an agreed period of time. Options trading is a facilitating contract and does not expressively require the investor to buy or sell or do both stocks and securities. The options market is the place or arena where buying and selling of options take place.

Types of Options

Options have two types called calls and puts. The call option allows you to buy shares or securities at a fixed price, which is known as the strike price. Options only last for a fixed period of time, and the option holder is not obligated to buy the shares or securities.

The put option allows you to sell shares or securities at a fixed price before a fixed date set as the expiration of the option. With this type of option also, you are not obligated to sell the shares or securities.

Writing an option is the process by which option traders create security through their selling actions and activities. By selling options, a security that was not in existence beforehand comes into existence. Writing an option is important to options trading because options are not issued the way stocks are issued by companies and exchanges; they only come into existence as a result of the activities of the options traders.

As an options trader, you can write a call or write a put. Writing a call means you want to sell shares or securities at a fixed price called the strike price before a fixed date known as the expiry date. Writing a call means you are interested in buying shares or securities at a fixed price before a fixed date known as the expiry date.

Styles of Options

The two basic options styles are the American style and the European style. The American style of options runs from the date the option becomes available (the date of purchase of the option) to the fixed date where the option expires. The European style of options is limited and does not offer time flexibility, as it can only be used on the expiry date.

Stock options and the majority of option-traded exchanges make use of the American style of options while the majority of index options make use of the European style of options.

Other Funds

Forex vs. Stocks

There are a few key differences between the forex market and the stock market. They differ in their volume, liquidity, time period, commission, and focus. There are also certain skills that must be possessed to trade properly. The trader must decide which is a better fit for them.

The forex market is much bigger, as there is approximately $5 trillion traded a day. This blows away the stock market, which trades about $200 billion per day. This means that the forex market has a much larger trading volume. Traders may have their orders executed more quickly and easily, and they may trade closer to their optimal prices. This also has an effect on the market's liquidity. This higher volume leads to higher liquidity. Higher liquidity means fewer gaps and lower transaction costs. Because of the greater volume, there will be more liquidity at each price point. Traders may more easily enter and exit the market and get the prices that they want. Forex is over-the-counter as opposed to a traditional exchange. This allows for trading to occur virtually whenever (typically 24 hours per day, five days per week). Normal stock trading hours are from 9:30 a.m. to 4:00 p.m. The extended hours may prove beneficial for those who work another job during that time or wish to do their trading at an uncommon hour. However, that also means that the trader must possibly subject themselves to more research, as there may be trading activity at any hour of the day, even during the nighttime. Forex traders typically do not have to worry about commission, as brokers profit off of the spread (the difference between the buying and selling price). Forex has a narrower focus, as there are eight major currencies to focus on. Stock, on the other hand, has thousands of possible trades. This means that there are many more options for what to trade, yet there is also a wider range of stock to educate oneself on and choose between.

The best option for the trader will also depend on the length of time that the trader wishes to invest for. Those who look to trade in the long-term may prefer stock trading, as the forex market tends to be more volatile. They may also enjoy the steady growth and dividends that stock gives. Those who trade forex for the long-term must also have large capital to cover such volatile movements. Those who prefer to swing-trade may choose either forex or stock. They should keep in mind, however, that trading forex may require more analysis because of the volatility. Those interested in day trading may prefer forex, as it is inexpensive to trade; however, there may be a requirement for large capital account balances for certain exchanges. The "better" choice will depend on the trader and their personal preferences.

Day Trading Futures

Some of the important things to consider about Day Trading futures include

1. There is no legal minimum starting capital required to begin Day Trading futures. Experts, however, recommend starting with $2,500 to $7,000 if one is trading the popular futures contract. The more money one starts with, the more flexible one will be when it comes to making trading decisions.

2. The official market hours for trading the S&P 500 and E-mini are from 9.30 am to 4 pm ET.

3. The optimal time to day trade ES futures is from 6.30 to 1030am and 3 to 4p Eastern time.

4. Commodities futures contracts also provide reliable Day Trading opportunities.

5. Most day traders who deal with futures often focus on one futures contract; however, others choose futures contracts seeing significant volume or movements on a particular day.

Exchange Traded Funds (ETFs)

These are a combination of stocks and mutual funds. Their benefit lies in their ability to give day traders access to market segments that would be extremely difficult to penetrate. What happens is that a money management firm buys a range of assets, such as stocks, bonds, and option, and then puts them together to create an ETF. The firm then lists this group of assets on the market for traders to purchase.

In order to trade in ETFs, you have to go to the large market indexes such as Dow Jones or S$P 500. ETFs are also available in many domestic bond indexes, foreign currencies, and international stock indexes.

How ETFs are traded

Day trading in ETFs is as simple as buying and selling stocks. You place an order through your brokerage firm and receive a price quote as well as a spread for the broker. The spread is simply the difference between the bid and the asking price. The bid price is the price that a broker buys stock from you, while the asking price is the price the broker charges you when you want to buy stock. The bid is lower than the asking price, and this is how the broker makes a profit.

ETFs can be traded on the NASDAQ and New York Stock Exchange.

Day trading with cryptocurrencies

A newer option you can choose for day trading is cryptocurrencies. These cryptocurrencies are taking over the world and many people are starting to notice. There are thousands of these currencies available and they offer security, anonymity, and a great way to make a profit if you use them the right way. And since their volatility is high, you can easily make a lot of profit in a short amount of time.

You have to be careful with this kind of investing though. There are no regulations on the currency and they are not available on the stock market. They also have a lot of ups and downs with them so it is also easy to lose your money quickly if you are not careful. You really need to do your due diligence here because, with so many options of cryptocurrencies to work with, many of them are not strong, and many can be fakes. And since these currencies are not regulated, you will not be able to get anyone to help you out if you pick the wrong type of currency.

Now, if you take the right precautions and are willing to watch the market to protect your money, cryptocurrencies can be perfect for earning money with day trading. In fact, after seeing the crash of Bitcoin in January 2018 after the currency reached almost $20,000 and then crashed to under $10,000 in a few days, investing in these currencies over the long-term is not the best. But the high volatility in these currencies makes them perfect to join into the cryptocurrency market, stay in for a few hours, and then get out and make a good profit in the process.

If you do decide to invest in cryptocurrencies, make sure that you take some time to research charts and the history of that currency. There will not be any reports from the SEC for you to read through and make informed decisions. Instead, you need to look online, read the charts, and learn the patterns of the currency on your own. But a smart investor who is willing to take the time and learn can make a big profit in no time.

Some cryptocurrencies, such as Bitcoin, are more established and can be great options to go with. Others are newer and you may need to do your research on as well. You also need to check the amount of variation that comes with the market. if you are only going to make a few dollars on a trade, it may not be worth your time. Just like with your broker, these cryptocurrency markets are going to charge you to exchange your fiat money with the cryptocurrency of your choice.

Chapter 10

What Kind of Day Trader are You

Day Trading

Day trading is an extremely involving strategy. Traders need to basically cancel all other engagements so they can focus on trading. This is because positions are often entered and exited in a matter of minutes and sometimes seconds. Losing focus for just a couple of minutes can cause a trader to lose money. Sometimes day traders are unable to stop for a moment or take a coffee break because day trading is so engaging. To newbies and beginners, it can be a daunting and sometimes even an arduous and insurmountable experience.

Day traders have to analyze the markets each and every single day. The analysis often happens early in the morning after waking up and just before the trading day begins. Day traders also need to choose a trading time-frame such as morning or afternoon sessions because the tasks are so demanding. It is almost impossible to switch between day trading and the TV.

Traders suffer from headaches and stress because of the constant vigil demanded. There are actually day traders who trade the entire day and are profitable. The challenge is that day trading is so demanding it takes traders away from regular activities like preparing lunch and so on.

Swing Trading

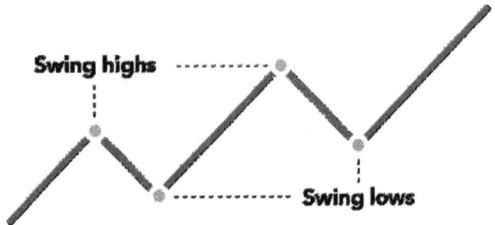

Swing trading is similar to long-term trend trailing, but instead, you are looking out for short market movements. Swinging trades usually last more than a single market day and may even extend for any time up to a few weeks. A swing trader is typically on the lookout for multi-day chart patterns. This precaution is because they attempt to make more significant price swings or moves than is generally gotten from day trading. The time frame employed on a chart by a forex swing trader usually varies from as long as an hour, as little as five minutes. A forex swing trader may employ the combination of technical analysis and fundamental analysis to direct their decisions. Whether the market is majorly range-bound or whether a long-term trend exists does not matter. A forex swing trader does not get to stay in a position long enough to have real damage. Volatility makes a lot of difference. A volatile market suits the forex swing trader well. The greater the volatility of the market, the higher the number of short-term price movements, and hence, the more the number of opportunities to perform a swing trade. Swing trading is perfect for the forex market for a variety of reasons, such as:

• That the market has enough volatility to capitalize on price moves.

• That you can take advantage of excellent liquidity.

• That you can achieve all this within a short time frame.

Trades done in a relatively short time frame demand constant supervision and monitoring. On the other hand, long-term trades require a lot of self-discipline. Most beginners go for swing trading because it uses a more appealing time frame. Here are some basic processes that will help as you swing trade:

• Follow the daily time frame: many traders spend most of their time on the daily charts. This method is because they provide a larger picture of what is occurring with the price actions and offer more reliable signs and pointers. But, all daily time frames are not exactly equal. It is therefore best, to begin with, the daily time frame. Once you become more skillful at swing trading, then you can move to the other time frames, like the 4-hour time frame. As a general principle, as you move to higher time frames from lower ones, price action signals become more trustworthy.

• Set vital resistance and support levels: this is a very crucial part of the entire swing trading process. Look at setting vital resistance and support levels as building the foundation of a house. It is impossible to locate favorable swing trades without their help. There are two types of levels: horizontal resistance and support and trend lines. The former is the most fundamental level that should be present on your charts. They provide a solid foundation for swing trading in the marketplace and provide some of the best target spaces. A swing trader should not ignore trend lines. They not only provide you with a means to locate entries with the trend but also serve to help identify reversals before they occur.

• Assess momentum: by the time you get to evaluating momentum, you must have fixed all relevant resistance and support areas and become familiar with the daily time frame. There are three main classes of market momentum, and they are: downtrend (lower lows and lower highs), uptrend (higher lows and higher highs), and range (sideways movement). A market that is on the downtrend is having lower lows and lower highs. On the other side of the spectrum, a market that is on the uptrend is having higher lows and higher highs. You should want to be a seller in a downtrend market and a buyer in an uptrend market. Then there is the ranging market. A ranging market happens when a market shifts sideways within a particular range. Although no bullish momentum exists, you can still make profitable swing trades. Some ranges are said to generate some of the best swing trades. This fact is because the resistance and support levels mostly stand out from the present price actions.

• Pay close attention to price action signs: You have understood how to identify vital resistance and support levels with the aid of the daily time frame. You also know how to assess the momentum of the market, so you can now identify and know the next step to take when the market is in a downtrend, range-bound, or in an upward trend. If the market is following an uptrend, then you should watch out for buy signs and signals from vital support. Some traders prefer candlestick patterns like the engulfing bar and the pin bar. On the other side of this, you may want to be on the lookout for sell signals and pointers from resistance when the market is on a downtrend. For example, signals like pin bars are used to locate the swing high, also known as the swing point. It is okay if you do not catch the entire swing. The main issue is to catch as much as you can, but it is crucial to wait to confirm price action. Be sure to examine your charts when looking for setups. Do not fall into the error of "searching" for setups. These two processes are dissimilar. Scanning for setups is more qualitative. Hence, you are scanning for the perfect setups, and if you find nothing, then it is fine. Many traders believe that they have to find a setup every time they look at their computer screen. This act is termed searching for setups. So scan for swing trade setups and do not go in search of them.

- Locate exit points: when it comes to locating exit points, there are two major rules to follow. The first rule is to decide on a profit target and fix a stop loss level. Some traders fall into the trap of only defining a target and do not remember that they also need their stop loss. Do not make this mistake. To calculate and monitor your risk, you need to have a well-defined stop loss level. The second rule is to establish both of these levels before you risk your capital. This period is the main time that you have a neutral bias. The moment you are at the risk of losing money, that neutral bias gets thrown off balance. You are therefore under pressure to put your exit points at levels that place your trades at an advantage, instead of placing your exit points based on what the market tells you.

- Examine and control risk: the next step after identifying your exit points using the right criteria is practicing risk management. When assessing the risk of a trade, you have to place the stop loss. For example, when using a pin bar, the perfect position is below or above the tail. The same as for a bearish or bullish engulfing pattern.

Forex Trading

Forex day trading is also known as intra-day trading. This strategy basically entails the buying and selling of foreign currencies. It also means that trades are opened and closed on the very same day. These kinds of trades are essentially full of action, so traders need to be present during the entire session.

Risks are often high when it comes to forex day trading, so traders have to be alert at all times. forex day trading rules are quite harsh, so close attention has to be paid when trades are made.

This refers to the purchase and sale of securities, but all this is done within the same trading day. forex day trading can happen in any market, but you need to fulfill some requirements in order to be successful at what you do. To succeed at forex day trading, you need to have enough capital and good knowledge of the market you plan to trade-in.

Most of the day traders opt for stocks because it eliminates the need for them to pay any fees just to keep a position alive overnight. However, this activity is highly speculative, though it keeps the market running smoothly. Forex day traders are responsible for providing the market with liquidity.

Day Trading in Forex

The media describe day trading as a simple task that you can do without the prerequisite knowledge, which is not the truth. As often suggested, this is not a get-rich-quick scheme that will take you from zero to well-off in just one day – you have to work to achieve your goal.

Here are the qualities of a successful Forex day trader:

Enough Capital Requirements

You need to have enough capital that you can handle risks properly. However, even with the large capital outlay, you still need to regulate the size of the trades.

Market Knowledge

Complete knowledge of the market - how it works and the major determining factors that determine the direction of the market are vital to any day trader. To be successful, you need to also understand how fundamental and technical indicators work.

Discipline

Every aspect of life requires a certain level of discipline, and trading is one of these. Lack of discipline in forex trading will lead to losses. Without discipline, you have a high chance of making losses time and time again. You need to come up with rules and make sure you follow them to the latter. Additionally, you need to be able to monitor prices for long periods without rushing to make decisions.

Have the Right Strategy

The right strategy allows you to run trades without experiencing huge losses. Trading conditions vary from day to day, which means that you do not need to stick to a specific strategy all day long. Be flexible enough so that you modify your strategy depending on the situation at hand.

How to be successful at Forex Day Trading

Forex day trading follows a similar trend the same as the other types of trades. First, you need to practice on the platform using a demo account. Use virtual money that the broker will provide before you can commit your real cash. It might sound simple but it is vital to cutting losses later. It is only through practice and understanding how forex works that you will be able to trade safely and make attractive profits.

Another point is to choose the right forex broker. Here, you need to consider among other things the cost of using the system and any expenses that you might incur when using the system. Before choosing a broker, make sure you research all their offers. Remember the cheaper the cost of placing trades, the more the benefits you stand to gain.

Some brokers give you a bonus when you deposit money using a certain mode, for instance using cryptocurrency. Always be on the lookout for offers from the broker so that you make the most out of your money.

When day trading Forex, you have a high probability of losing your investment, it is therefore advisable that you only use money that you can lose. Although the Forex market gives you a high level of leverage, you need to remember that this leverage comes with a high possibility of losses and profit. Always follow the rules that you set and do not overtrade.

You also need to understand the different types of charts and how they work. Know which chart works where and why you need them in the first place.

How Often should You Day Trade Forex?

Before you decide how many times to place trades each day, you first need to have a strategy. The strategy is the one that will guide you in making decisions. For instance, place trade amounts depending on what you have set down in the strategy. Below are some rules that you can follow to help you with forex trading:

- Monday is not a very good day to place trades, because a lack of liquidity can make the market move sharply in any direction.
- One of the best markets to trade on is London. Here, a single trade can make your day and give you all the profits you need for the day.
- Breakout trading works when a stock reaches a maximum or minimum.
- The last hour of trading is important for the day because it tells you how strong the trend is. The trend might even continue the next day if nothing else happens.
- Avoid trading on late Fridays or on bank holidays.

- The first hour is vital to establishing the framework for the rest of the day.

The Mindset of the Day Trader

Willing to Play above the Line

The successful day trader knows and understands that he or she need to be responsible for any action they undertake in the trading. Rather than putting blame on anything and everything, try and be accountable for the actions and trading decisions you take.

Remember that every market is the same, only a lot of terrible trading decisions made by traders. If you find that the market you thought was great has become untradeable. Then you can change to a different market. Alternatively, you can adopt a different trading approach. As a trader, you have very many things that you can do to turn things around.

Have the Right Attitude

Trading can be easy and simple, or very tough depending on how you regard it. Along the path of trading, you encounter losses, but this does not mean you give up because each day is not the same.

To succeed, focus on going after your goals and forget the negatives. It is vital that you stay positive always.

Are Honest

Things can happen when you trade on a daily basis. Did you trade emotionally this week? Did you go out of your strategy? Well, you need to be honest and stick to your plan and take the blame when you make decisions that did not add to your goals.

High Levels of Commitment

Trading success does not come overnight – it needs you to be committed and put in a lot of effort each day. Many traders lose out on trades because they thought that they know everything about trading only for them to come up short. They got into the market with the mentality that they will use a "magic" system that does everything for them without having to commit their resources.

Trading is similar to any other line of work, you have to gain knowledge of a few fundamentals, apply them, and then achieve experience before you improve your trade. Remember that learning is unending, and with constant learning, you end up with the right experience.

Winning vs. Losing Day Traders

The very fine line that separates these two types of day traders is the mindset. In particular, the day trading mindset involves behavior and emotions.

One of the reasons why a lot of day traders fail in this industry is the way they take trading losses and other negative trading-related developments, i.e., they take these things very personally. This means that their self-esteem and inner peace are hijacked by the results of their trades. If they execute winning trades, they feel great about themselves and experience inner peace. When they execute losing ones, they feel inferior or insecure and become very anxious.

This is a very bad thing because trading is about numbers and numbers are objective. People cannot master something objective by using emotions. Losing day traders tend to react on how they feel because of the results of their trades while winning ones tend to look at their losing trades objectively and from a constructive perspective.

Remember the trading experience I shared earlier. Keep that in mind as a very strong case for keeping emotions under control if you want to experience a generally successful day trading career. While you may not win each and every trade, being objective can help you increase the odds of executing more winning trades than losing ones.

Do you want to know how many of the world's most successful day traders deal with their emotions, especially in light of the results of their own day trades?

Focusing on Skills Rather Than Profits

One, they trade with the primary goal of becoming better and better at it. The money's just secondary. By focusing on getting better at their day trading skills, they feel they win with every trade, regardless of the result. If they execute profitable trades, they win in monetary terms. When they lose, they still feel like winners because they look at such trades as profitable lessons on how to trade better the next time.

Ignoring Profit and Loss Records During Trading Hours

Another way winning traders keep their emotions in check enough to consistently execute winning trades is by ignoring their trading profits and losses records DURING trading. They do this so that they do not get emotionally riled up by the cumulative results of their trade.

You may be wondering: If winning day traders do not pay attention to their profits and losses during trading hours, how can they keep their trading losses in check?

They do so by doing something along the lines of the three-step day trading risk management technique. Because they already set profit-taking and stop-loss limits per trade, they can focus on trading knowing that such limits, which are programmed into most day trading programs and platforms, will keep them from losing more than what they intended to.

Because they have already set up automated profit-taking and stop-loss limits, they are free to focus more on effectively executing their day trading strategies. And by hiding their day trading profit and loss records during trading hours, they minimize the risk of becoming emotional while day trading.

Self-Discipline

Another key difference between winning and losing traders is self-discipline. Winning day traders are disciplined enough to stick to their trading strategies in case of hell or high water, e.g., profit-taking and stop-loss price levels, trading amounts, etc. Losing day traders are usually an undisciplined bunch that bases their trades on "gut feel" or their moods. On some days, they trade less than their maximum risk tolerance while on some days, they trade exceedingly more.

There are two important factors that can significantly impact your ability to exercise the necessary amount of self-discipline for successful day trading: physical and mental health.

Physical health is influenced by three very important things: nutrition, regular exercise, and rest. There is a saying that we are what we eat. If we eat junk food, we get junk bodies that easily breakdown and deteriorate. When we eat mostly healthy food, we get healthy bodies.

Eating the right kinds of food also affects our energy level throughout the day, which can have a huge impact on our ability to think and make quick decisions. You will have a hard time making very objective decisions quickly if you feel lethargic, sluggish, or foggy, which is highly likely if you eat a lot of highly-processed and sugary foods. But if you eat mostly complex carbs and high-quality protein, you can enjoy steady energy levels throughout the day, which can help you think clearly and quickly.

Regular exercise can help increase your energy levels throughout the day and make you feel more alert. These can help you stick to your day trading strategies, think more clearly, and make decisions faster, which are all important when you are trying to take timely positions on securities while day trading. When you do not get enough regular exercise, you will most likely feel sluggish or agitated because of all the unreleased energy in your body.

Finally, you cannot feel energetic enough and think clearly and fast enough when you chronically lack sleep. Sluggishness and brain fog are two of the worst enemies of day traders, especially when markets are moving very fast. Try to get as much sleep as you can every night if you really want to do well in day trading.

Mental health, believe it or not, is also largely influenced by the same three things that influence physical health. The kinds of foods you eat, your ability to get regular exercise in, and getting enough sleep to contribute to optimal mental health and consequently, cognitive performance.

Going back to the topic of self-discipline, you will need it to continue trading and get enough practice to eventually make more winning day trades than losing ones. Remember, day trading is a skill that can be mastered but skill mastery requires a lot of practice time. Without self-discipline, you will not be able to hang around long enough to enjoy the fruits of your day trading practice.

Chapter 11

Managing Risk in Trading and the Role of Journaling

The first thing you need to know as a trader is that you will run volumes of trades and experience a lot of risks. Trading the markets is one of the riskiest investment techniques, and many people go for day trading because they have the potential for higher gains over a short period. If you have a small account, day trading gives you the chance to grow small accounts in such a short timeframe.

Risk comes about because you have to execute hundreds of trades in such a short time. You also have the capacity to place any trade you want, for as low as $500 or as high as $25,000 in a single trade. The trades are also at high speed, which means the market can swing any way – up or down. The direction of the market determines whether you make a loss or a profit.

Day trading gives you two realms of strategies to go with – high-risk trading strategies or Lowe risk strategies. The goal of a successful trader is to maximize profit while lowering risks. Every time you place a trade, you need to evaluate the risk of the trade and then weigh it against the potential reward. Often times this is made worse by our emotional reaction to various price directions. For instance, since you experienced a loss recently, the next logical step would be to take a higher risk on the next trade so that you can compensate for the loss. Experienced traders have a heightened level of awareness that they use to recognize a loss and reward and will make sure they take the right decision. However, you have to learn the skill over time.

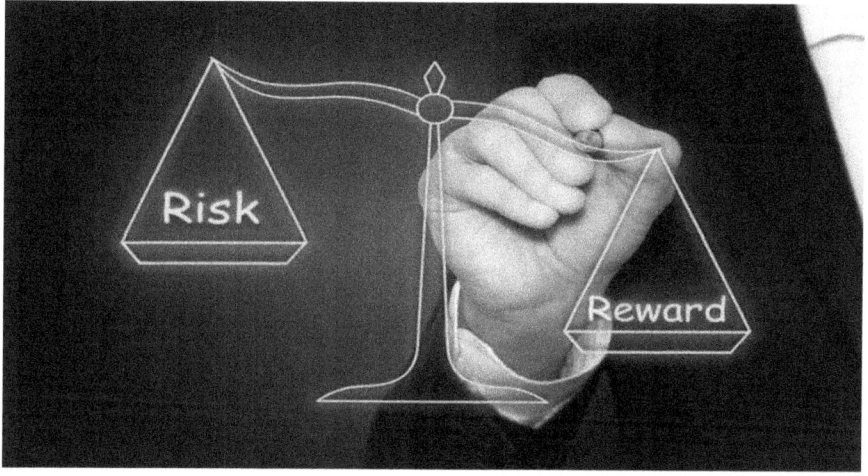

You can develop a sense of decision making by keeping a journal as you trade and then reviewing the notes after the close of the market.

Different Types of risk

When talking about risk, you need to consider the different types in order for you to understand what we are saying. As a day trader, your primary role is to know the distance between the entry and the stop. Stop loss needs to be based on a resistance area on the chart or recent support.

The majority of your losses happen when a trade hits the stop price. This means you will not make any profit on whatever you are trading.

The second type of risk is the volatility of the market. As day traders, volatility is a friend to all of us, but it is also risky because markets that are extremely volatile tend to result in higher losses than what you actually planned for. Since there is a sense of inherent risk in trading, you need to try and avoid placing a trade when the volatility cannot be predicted, for instance when there is breaking news.

The other type of risk is exposure risk. Exposure results when you multiply the price of shares by the number of held shares. As an investor, you increase this risk when you hold on positions for a very long time. To mitigate this risk, you need to hold onto shares for a short time.

If you are holding onto large positions for a long time you stand to experience stock halts. Halts can take hours or days, though they are rare. The most common halts are those waiting for the release of news or volatility halts. Anytime a stock halts, it can lead to a different price. The biggest risk is that the stock might reopen at a very different price, which might be lower than the current price of the stock. You can take steps to reduce the effect of the halts by understanding what leads to the halts in the first place.

Journaling

If you are looking at a routine that is easy to implement and that can change the way you trade, then think about keeping a journal. The journal is a little black book that details what you do each day.

The aim of keeping a journal is to help improve your setups so that you use your experiences to analyze and help refine your trading while you improve the whole experience.

Here, we look at all you need to come up with a journal and maintain it.

1. What is A Journal?

A trading journal is a way to keep track of what you are doing on a daily basis as a day trader. You jot down notes of what you do each day especially the different trades (or lack of) and the results of any action you take.

The trading journal needs to be tailored to your trading styles and preferences. You can keep the journal in a physical notebook or a detailed digital document on your computer. Regardless of the format, when maintained with due diligence, the trading journal can be the best way to make you a better day trader.

2. How Does the Trading Journal Help You Achieve Better Trades?

There are a number of ways in which a trading journal will help you become better at what you do.

Many traders attribute their success in creating and maintaining a trading journal. By noting down the different trades, you are able to check the progress over time. This allows you to find out what is working or not and change or modify them to succeed.

Helps You develop discipline in Trading

Having a trading journal helps you develop discipline as you trade. How does it work? Well, it forces you to follow the guidelines that you have set down.

The sense of accountability that you get when you have a trading journal makes sure you are responsible for research and trading. If you know what you need to keep a log each day, you do it without failing. Making sure you log your trades and whatever happens, requires a lot of discipline. Good habits such as these require you to go straight when executing trades.

Helps You Master Your Emotions

One of the top suggestions to help you run trades the right way is to trade like you are not human. Machines do not have emotions and approach all the processes in a scientific way.

However, this is much easier to say than to do. When you get in a position to lose money, usually you find it tough getting emotion out of the way.

Keeping a journal can help you keep the emotions out of the way. With a journal in place, you get to keep track of how you feel emotionally in various trading stages. This is just to keep the emotions under control.

With time, you realize that there is a pattern that is emerging, for instance, you might find yourself getting calmer and trade the right way each time.

Improves Your Risk Management Practices

Day trading comes with a high level of risk. This is something that you cannot change at all because it is the nature of the market for things to run this way. However, there are various ways in which you can mitigate these risks. For one, you need to invest a large amount of research and study to give you the knowledge that you need to choose the least risky trades possible.

With a journal, you can learn things about risk tolerance. For instance, you might find that you have consistently been able to hold positions for longer and you have been losing profits as a result. You might also find that you have issues getting out of trades because you have been taking positions that are too big for your stage.

By looking at the risks that you have been taking and how they affect the results you return, you get to make adjustments.

For instance, you might exit trades sooner or you might end up taking smaller positions based on the results you return. This way you help reduce risks and improve risk management.

Creating the Perfect Trading Diary

Now that you know how effective the trading journal is, you need to know how to come up with the best one. Here are a few tips for success when coming up with a journal:

- Be consistent

Trading needs you to have a routine. You will probably get the most out of the journal if you have a routine that you follow religiously.

You also need to follow the latter routine. This means that you are consistent with what you do day after day. For instance, you need to wake up early each day to prepare for trading. This allows you to get errands and tasks out of the way early and gives you to do research so that you are ready to roll when the market starts.

This is a directive though because since many traders are doing other responsibilities, you need to come up with the right schedule that works for you. Choose the routine that will work for you and that you can stick to easily.

- Analyze the Market

The more the trades that you track, the more data you have to deal with, the more you get to learn the faster you do it.

By recording the trades, overall thoughts, market observations, and more, you are not just learning from the mistakes that you are doing, but you are also gaining a sense of how to perform the right market analysis.

For instance, with the right trading data, you get to notice gains and losses in a particular industry or sector. This can give you clues on the trends in the market that you might have missed out on.

Once you see what is working and what is not, you get to have a targeted market analysis.

- Analyze and Come Up with Your Own Setups

A trading journal allows you to come up with the right setups. Here is how this works out:

- Find the setups that trigger trade entry

When do you enter the market? The trading journal helps you figure everything out. You need to go into each trade with a plan. However, if you realize that you are entering trades too soon or too late based on the journal, you can then decide to try something different.

With the perfect trading journal, you have the capacity to determine the setups that trigger the entries.

- Gain Insight into the Market

When you record your own setups, you have the ability to gain insight into the market that you are trading in. You get to notice market trends and how they might end up affecting the setups.

As a trader, understanding the way the market runs is ideal because it helps you to keep up to date. The market is dynamic, and the setups that work in one market condition might not work for other conditions. When you understand the market, you get to navigate around and acclimatize to new markets.

- Know the Appropriate Lot Size

In any market, the lot size means the number of shares that you buy in any transaction. The theory of size allows you to regulate price quotes. It is basically the size of the trade that you place in the financial market.

With price regulation being a part of every market, you need to always be aware of the number of units that you purchase on contract, and determine the price you pay per unit.

Make sure you keep track of the lot sizes that you deal with in any trade, as it helps you to decide the types of approaches that you take in the future.

- Determine the Style of Trading

Many traders choose to be one type of trader than another. Many of them do it by force, which is a fact that is not the best. As a trader, you need to naturally gravitate towards a specific trading style, and not force it.

Rather than chasing after what is trendy or what you have seen other traders do, it is advisable to focus on a style of trading that gives you profit, whether you go after long or short positions.

A trading journal can help you determine the type of trade that is best suited for you by giving a summary of the trades that gave you money.

- Understand Profit Placement

Trading is a probability game, with so many moving pieces that make it work. With so many parts that are needed to make everything work, you need to make sure you get everything right the first time. This is not easy at all.

Here are a few specifics that you need to master:

- *Cut losses fast*: you need to learn to cut losses quickly, which means you pull out of a position earlier than later, even if it means missing out on a few profits. It is always good to be safe than sorry. Having a trading journal helps you determine when to get out of a trade. If you notice that you are losing constantly, then journaling can help you learn how to cut losses fast.

Additionally, if you notice that you are getting out of trades too early, then you can start staying in the game a little bit longer.

- *Stop losses*: you need to learn how to come up with the best stop-loss order. The order can help you release the order when you reach a particular price. With the right stop-loss order, you can buy the security rather than selling it when you reach a certain price. Make sure you record the different entry and exit positions; how much you have risked and the results of everything. As the information collects over time, you can determine what your best setups are so that you can focus on replicating the profits you gained in the past to eliminate losses.

Apart from this information, you also need to record other things so that you make the most out of each entry:

- *The date*: this should not be left out of the journal. Not only does it help you to track what you were doing and when you were doing it, but it allows you to go back and look at the performance of the stock on that date in the future. Never assume that you will rack everything in your brain!

- *The Time Frame*: do not just record the date, but make sure you know the perfect time for each entry. In the world of trading, minutes matter. Trading in the morning can make a huge difference compared to trading in the afternoon. For instance, the setup that works for you during the morning hours might not work the same way in the afternoon.

- *Price in*: this is the point where the journal starts working well with the trading plan. When coming up with a trading plan, you set the key tactics such as the entry point, the exit, and what you plan to gain from this trade. This helps you to stick to the plan and then keep emotions out of things. In the journal, make sure you note the price at which you entered a successful trade.

- *Price out*: do not just mark the time that you entered the trade – also take note of the price that you exit the trade too. The exit is also as vital as the entrance. Keeping this data allows you to analyze whether you are staying in a position for the right amount of time. Note any difficulties that you encounter getting out of the position, as this might affect the level of risk next time.

- *Amount you are risking*: before you enter a trade, you need to determine the amount of money you plan to put into the trade. Note: The money you put in should be an amount you can risk losing. So, how much money should you risk on a trade? The answer is that you need to always take a cautious position, and never try to risk what you cannot lose. You do not want to enter into a trade and blow up the account as this might trigger emotional trading.

Tips for Creating an Efficient Trading Journal

Identify the Patterns That lead to Losses

As a trader, you cannot eliminate the risk of making losses. For many traders, the success rate is 70 percent, and many of them know that the 100 percent win rate is a myth.

You can never control how much you win, but you can at least control the amount you can lose by cutting losses fast.

You also get to learn from the losses. Once you have a trading journal, you begin to identify patterns that lead to losses and assess what is happening.

Identify the Patterns That Have Made You Profit

Being a trader, you not only have to focus on the things that went wrong but also look at what went right as well. You need to chart patterns in the trades to help you analyze what makes you the most money. Many successful traders base their success on being able to identify patterns. Many depend on stock charts, but later realize that even the trading journal gives them an insight into what they need to do.

Go for Professional Assistance

Trading classes give you an asset that you will never regret in your trading life. Even with the right data, you might find yourself failing to make profitable trades because you do not have the mechanics to make things work for you. When you take the time to learn the mechanics of trading, you find that you have the basis to identify key indicators and add them to the journal.

Just like any other trade, the more you get prepared to execute trades the more successful you become. The knowledge originates from previous traders that have become successful in their efforts

Work With templates

Templates make it easy for you to come up with a plan. There are many platforms online that offer you both paid and free templates that you can use to create the perfect journal, all you need to do is to choose the one that suits you most and then customize it to your liking. As you become more adept, you find that the journal becomes your best friend, and it also becomes more detailed.

Chapter 12

Tips for Market Investing

Maximizing Your Investments

There are several ways that investors may maximize their investments. Of course, practicing proper trading techniques will help investors to earn greater returns on their investments. However, there are several other ways in which investors may maximize their investments and improve the returns on those investments. They may decrease investment costs, increase diversification, rebalance, and practice other techniques to improve their investments. It is important to learn about all the possible ways to maximize one's investments because you do not know what you do not know. Every bit counts. Just saving a bit here and there will quickly add up and maximize the investments.

Investors may maximize their investments by decreasing the cost of investing. There are several ways that investing may cost money, and that money is coming directly out of the investment. Investors may switch from hiring a financial advisor or doing the investing themselves, cutting the costs of commission. Investors commonly forget about transaction costs. There is typically a flat fee for buying stock through a broker. Instead of making many small purchases, investors may save up and only buy stocks in certain increments (for example, perhaps the investor will not buy more stocks until he or she has saved $1000). By doing this, a much smaller percentage of the investment is being cut out and used to cover those fees. This may require more patience, but that money will add up. Lowering one's expenses will increase their return. Instead of being spent, that money may be growing and earning a return on it. Because of compound interest, this money will earn money on itself and multiply over a period of years. This is why it is crucial to save every bit possible.

Investors must also really pay attention to their portfolios. Diversification is crucial, and it can save the investor from losing all of their investment. Markets typically fall much more quickly than markets rise. This means that the investor must prepare for such occurrences. It is important to regularly rebalance one's portfolio to ensure that it is positioned correctly for the investor to make the largest possible gains.

Investors must also truly pay attention to what they want. Maximizing one's investments will depend on the person and what their goals are. Although it is wise to listen to the advice of experts and see what other ways that one may invest, it is crucial to follow the path that is best for the goals and preferences of the individual. This is why a plan is necessary and should be followed. Investors must not stop investing. This is another way to take advantage of compound interest. The investor's portfolio should never stop growing. This growth should be due to both growths in the investment and regular contributions by the investor themselves. Despite the great returns that may be experienced in a bull market, contributions are still necessary. Bear markets should also not discourage investors from continuing to invest; this can be a great time to get a good deal on a stock!

Retirement Plans

There are several savings plans that investors can get involved with. These can help to provide the investor with additional benefits that would not be available to them otherwise.

One of these plans is a 401(k). This is a retirement savings plan that will be sponsored by an employer. This will allow the individual to invest their money before taxes so that they can save and invest some of their paychecks. The investor is not required to pay taxes until they withdraw this money from their account. Investors may control how to invest their money. It is common to have mutual funds that contain stocks, bonds, and money market investments. However, there are also target-date funds, which are stocks and bonds that will decrease in risk as the investor nears their retirement age. Unlike individual investing, however, this plan may not offer its users complete freedom. For instance, most employees must work for a company for a certain period of time before gaining access to their payments. Employees may even have to work for the company for a certain period of time before being able to enroll in a 401(k) at all. There are typical costs for withdrawing from these accounts before hitting retirement age as well. There are also contribution limits for each year. Investing for oneself, however, offers more freedom, and there are no limits on investing. For those working for an employer, however, this may be a good solution investing using the paycheck given. It is a way to utilize the ability not to be taxed on one's investments from their paycheck. Employees may also enroll in Roth 401(k)s, which are not taxed for withdrawals. The better choice will depend on both the employee and the employer, as the plans are taxed differently.

The 403(b) plans are similar to 401(k)s, yet there are some slight differences. Both offer matching of the investments. For instance, for every dollar the employee contributes, the employer may contribute $0.50. This can prove to be greatly helpful to investors. The major difference between these is the employees that may enroll in these plans. Those in public schools, government jobs, nonprofits, and more may register for this plan. They are not for private-sector workers. Besides this, the plans are identical in their purposes. A 403(b) plan, however, may allow for faster vesting of funds and additional contributions, although the investment options may be less plentiful.

There are also IRA plans. These are plans to save for retirement. These plans have different contribution limits, tax rules, and penalties for early withdrawals. Traditional IRAs are plans that are set up to save for retirement by the individual instead of by a company. The owner of the account will make contributions to the account. To open an account, the individual must have earned income during the year and be under 70.5 years of age. Simple IRAs are set up by small business owners for their employees. Both the owner of the account and their employee will contribute. To open an account, the employee must follow any rules set by their employer. Roth IRAs do not give a tax break when contributing, yet the retirement withdrawals are typically tax-free. Those wishing to enroll in such a plan should research their options. If given the option, the individual should research the pros and cons of their options and decide which will provide them with the best way to reach their goals. Some may not have the option given to them, yet it is wise to educate oneself on where their money is going. This may help to allow the individual to see more ways to maximize their investments.

The Importance Of Retirement Planning

The importance of retirement planning can never be overemphasized. This is because there is nothing more important in life as having a well -prepared retirement plan. Now a day cause of the elevated technology, we cannot be blamed for thinking of short-term goals like big-screen TVs, rather than getting ready for our futures. We are always coming up with excuses and explanations on why we delay these preparations and before we realize it, age catches up with us and it is suddenly too late to start planning.

Retirement planning, as we have already seen starts with setting life goals that are clearly defined and assembling a financial plan that will enable you to achieve your goals after retirement. Planners must start planning early on so as to benefit from compound interest and also to steer clear of financial risk. The highest risk to a well-planned retirement is the possibility of living longer than your money.

Those who have had the misfortune of outliving their retirement funds have repeatedly found themselves living in absolute poverty or working until the day of their death. Others who depended wholly on the Social Security system have found it to be such disarray, and it is therefore wise not to depend entirely on this money. As a matter of fact, even Social Security is advising us not to count on it. According to financial experts, Social Security funds will only be able to cater for not more than 40% of the money the average person will need to live on upon retirement. That, to say the least, is a dreadful situation, but one that we will all have to live with unless we start planning for the future in a sensible manner.

After all, there is absolutely no reason why you must be caught unawares. The sooner you start planning, the sooner you will be able to relax, and the better it will be for you and those that you love. Seeing that you are bound to retire as one day, you must acknowledge the exact goals you wish to achieve in life.

On the other hand, if you have a spouse or next of kin, both of you should convene, exchange information and cooperate to make sure that what you are working at is what you both want eventually. The normal goals in life include creating families, studying hard so as to receive higher education degrees and setting money aside so as to leave your descendants well provided for, or to engage in charitable causes.

Direct Stock Purchase Plans

Direct stock purchase plans allow investors to directly purchase stock from the company without the use of a broker. These plans may be available directly to retail investors, yet some companies will use third-party administrators to handle the transactions. They will typically have lower fees and the potential for buying shares at a discounted price. This may not be an option for all companies. These plans may also come with restrictions on when the investor may purchase shares.

This, plan may attract long-term investors who do not have sufficient funds for an initial investment.

The investor may choose to sign up once for this plan, or they may sign up to make automatic and periodic investments through a transfer agent. This agent will maintain balances and record transactions. To keep costs low, transfer agents will typically carry out bulk transactions for the company each time and period that they choose. Direct stock purchase plans are an alternative to using online brokerages, and they will typically cost less. Instead of paying higher transaction fees, the investor may pay a small purchase processing fee for each share that they purchase. These are usually quite a bit smaller than the transaction fees that investors must pay a brokerage. This means that the investor will have more money that they will be able to invest in. Instead of giving the money to the brokerage, that money may be invested and generate a return for the investor. This can prove to be a wise move, especially for those wishing to buy a lesser amount of stocks. For those with greater funds for trading stocks, an online brokerage may prove more beneficial for the individual.

Direct stock purchase plans are not for everyone. They will typically require investors to make a certain monthly commitment (i.e., $100) to investing. On the other hand, investors may buy stocks from a brokerage once and never buy it again. Investors will also have to pay the market price for their stocks instead of being able to time it themselves. It may also be less convenient to create another account. However, once you started, this will be an automatic investment and will not cost as much as it would purchase stocks through a broker.

This plan works by the investor making monthly deposits and those deposits being put towards purchasing shares of the company's stock. New shares (or portions of shares) will be purchased each month based on the amount of money available from deposits and dividends. This is a simple way to acquire shares of a company's stock slowly. This is also inexpensive, as these plans typically have either low costs or no costs at all. They also have low minimum deposits, usually ranging from about $100 to $500, although this may vary. This is a great plan for those who lack the financial power to invest otherwise. A common way that these purchase plans are carried out is by combining them with dividend reinvestment plans. These may be combined with the direct stock purchase plans to maximize the amount that the investor is investing in.

Dividend Reinvestment Plans

Dividend reinvestment plans allow investors to, as the name suggests, reinvest their dividends. These are typically free to sign up for and quite easy to get started in. Investors must simply check a box or click a few buttons to sign up, and the dividends that they earn will go towards reinvesting into shares of stocks. Perhaps the investor gets a dividend for stock x. If they have signed up for DRIP (Dividend Reinvestment Plan), that dividend will go towards shares (or portions of shares) of purchasing more of stock x. This is a great way to manage one's investments automatically. On the dividend payment date, the investor's dividend will go towards reinvesting in that stock.

There are ways to sign up for this through the brokerage that one trades through or through an investment company. Instead of taking out these dividends and spending them, they may be used for greater benefits to the investor. These dividends can help the investor to make more money. Instead of receiving a check or depositing it into the investor's bank, this money may be reinvested into buying more stocks. The investor should keep in mind, however, that these shares will be bought at market price and will typically be bought directly from the company, which is why this is free of transaction costs. Also, these shares will not be marketable through stock exchanges; they must be redeemed through the company directly.

There may be some limitations to this. Although these may be commission-free for the investor and may even have discounted share prices, DRIPs may have minimum dollar amounts that must be invested. There may be a minimum purchase amount for this. This is a great way for investors to take advantage of compound interest, as they are adding the extra amount that they may not have invested otherwise. However, the dividends may still be taxable, and the shares will be illiquid. The investor, once they have signed up, will not be able to regulate how much is and is not reinvested from these dividends. It is also a great way for investors to increase

Conclusion

Let's hope it was informative and able to provide you with all of the tools you need to achieve your goals whatever they may be.

The next step is to first try trading options on paper. This way, you will be able to visualize actual trades without losing any money. Try and build your confidence this way and then move to an online trade simulator. Here, you will trade just like you would on a broker's platform. However, you will use virtual money. It is only after you are thoroughly versed with options trading, including common terminology, trading strategies, and so on that, you can now sign up with a broker and open a trading account. If you follow the instructions in this book, then you will begin making good profits in no time. Options are very lucrative and can make you wealthy if applied well.

I want to take a moment before we part ways to celebrate you for investing the time in learning how to conduct trades. Trading can be an intimidating topic, but as you may notice by now it is certainly not challenging to engage in once you know what you are doing. Although the stakes may seem higher because they involve cash money, the general consensus remains the same: as long as you continue to educate yourself on how to make this strategy work and you continue honing your skills, it will become easier.

www.ingramcontent.com/pod-product-compliance
Lightning Source LLC
Chambersburg PA
CBHW070646220526
45466CB00001B/309